FIRST PAST THE POST

English:

Comprehensions

Classic Literature

Book 2

© 2019 ElevenPlusExams.co.uk COPYING STRICTLY PROHIBITED

How to use this book to make the most of 11 plus exam preparation

It is important to remember that for 11 plus exams there is no national syllabus, no pass mark and no retake option. It is therefore vital that your child is fully primed to perform to the best of their ability so that they give themselves the best possible chance on the day.

Unlike similar publications, the **First Past The Post®** series uniquely assesses your child's performance on a question-by-question basis, helping to identify areas for improvement and providing suggestions for further targeted tests. By entering the unique Peer-Compare™ access code for this book on our website, your child's performance can be compared anonymously to that of others who have taken the same tests.

Comprehensions: Classic Literature

This collection of tests is representative of the standard comprehension section of contemporary multi-discipline 11 plus and Common Entrance exams. Questions test the student's ability to extract factual information or draw inferences from the text, and some test the student's knowledge of vocabulary, grammar or literary techniques. All passages in this book are taken from classic fiction books, such as those by Wilkie Collins and Anna Sewell.

The suggested time for each test is based on data obtained from classroom-testing sessions held at our centre.

Never has it been more useful to learn from mistakes!

Students can improve by as much as 15%, not only by focused practice, but also by targeting any weak areas.

How to manage your child's practice

To get the most up-to-date information, visit our website, www.elevenplusexams.co.uk, the UK's largest online resource for 11 plus, with over 65,000 webpages and a forum administered by a select group of experienced moderators.

About the authors

The Eleven Plus Exams' **First Past The Post®** series has been created by a team of experienced tutors and authors from leading British universities.

Published by Technical One Ltd t/a Eleven Plus Exams

With special thanks to all the children who tested our material at the ElevenPlusExams centre in Harrow.

ISBN: 978-1-912364-03-9

Copyright © ElevenPlusExams.co.uk 2019

Second edition

All rights reserved. No part of this publication may be reproduced, stored or introduced into a retrieval system or transmitted in any form or by any means, without the prior written permission of the publisher nor may be circulated in any form of binding or cover other than the one in which it was published and without a similar condition including this condition being imposed on the subsequent publisher.

About Us

At Eleven Plus Exams, we supply high-quality 11 plus tuition for your children. Our free website at **www.elevenplusexams.co.uk** is the largest website in the UK that specifically prepares children for the 11 plus exams. We also provide online services to schools and our **First Past The Post®** range of books has been well-received by schools, tuition centres and parents.

Eleven Plus Exams is recognised as a trusted and authoritative source. We have been quoted in numerous national newspapers, including *The Telegraph*, *The Observer*, the *Daily Mail* and *The Sunday Telegraph*, as well as on national television (BBC1 and Channel 4), and BBC radio.

Our website offers a vast amount of information and advice on the 11 plus, including a moderated online forum, books, downloadable material and online services to enhance your child's chances of success. Set up in 2004, the website grew from an initial 20 webpages to more than 65,000 today, and has been visited by millions of parents. It is moderated by experts in the field, who provide support for parents both before and after the exams.

Don't forget to visit **www.elevenplusexams.co.uk** and see why we are the market's leading one-stop shop for all your 11 plus needs. You will find:

- ✓ Comprehensive quality content and advice written by 11 plus experts
- ✓ Eleven Plus Exams online shop supplying a wide range of practice books, e-papers, software and apps
- ✓ Lots of FREE practice papers to download
- ✓ Professional tuition service
- ✓ Short revision courses
- ✓ Year-long 11 plus courses
- ✓ Mock exams tailored to reflect those of the main examining bodies

Other Titles in the First Past The Post® Series
11+ Essentials Range of Books

978-1-912364-60-2	Verbal Reasoning: Cloze Tests Book 1 - Mixed Format
978-1-912364-61-9	Verbal Reasoning: Cloze Tests Book 2 - Mixed Format
978-1-912364-78-7	Verbal Reasoning: Cloze Tests Book 3 - Mixed Format
978-1-912364-79-4	Verbal Reasoning: Cloze Tests Book 4 - Mixed Format
978-1-912364-62-6	Verbal Reasoning: Vocabulary Book 1 - Multiple Choice
978-1-912364-63-3	Verbal Reasoning: Vocabulary Book 2 - Multiple Choice
978-1-912364-64-0	Verbal Reasoning: Vocabulary Book 3 - Multiple Choice
978-1-912364-65-7	Verbal Reasoning: Vocabulary, Spelling and Grammar Book 1 - Multiple Choice
978-1-912364-66-4	Verbal Reasoning: Vocabulary, Spelling and Grammar Book 2 - Multiple Choice
978-1-912364-68-8	Verbal Reasoning: Vocabulary in Context Level 1
978-1-912364-69-5	Verbal Reasoning: Vocabulary in Context Level 2
978-1-912364-70-1	Verbal Reasoning: Vocabulary in Context Level 3
978-1-912364-71-8	Verbal Reasoning: Vocabulary in Context Level 4
978-1-912364-74-9	Verbal Reasoning: Vocabulary Puzzles Book 1
978-1-912364-75-6	Verbal Reasoning: Vocabulary Puzzles Book 2
978-1-912364-76-3	Verbal Reasoning: Practice Papers Book 1 - Multiple Choice
978-1-912364-77-0	Verbal Reasoning: Practice Papers Book 2 - Multiple Choice

978-1-912364-02-2	English: Comprehensions Classic Literature Book 1 - Multiple Choice
978-1-912364-03-9	English: Comprehensions Classic Literature Book 2 - Multiple Choice
978-1-912364-05-3	English: Comprehensions Contemporary Literature Book 1 - Multiple Choice
978-1-912364-06-0	English: Comprehensions Contemporary Literature Book 12- Multiple Choice
978-1-912364-08-4	English: Comprehensions Non-Fiction Book 1 - Multiple Choice
978-1-912364-09-1	English: Comprehensions Non-Fiction Book 2 - Multiple Choice
978-1-912364-23-7	English: Comprehensions Poetry Book 1 - Multiple Choice
978-1-912364-14-5	English: Mini Comprehensions - Inference Book 1
978-1-912364-15-2	English: Mini Comprehensions - Inference Book 2
978-1-912364-16-9	English: Mini Comprehensions - Inference Book 3
978-1-912364-11-4	English: Mini Comprehensions - Fact-Finding Book 1
978-1-912364-12-1	English: Mini Comprehensions - Fact-Finding Book 2
978-1-912364-21-3	English: Spelling, Punctuation and Grammar Book 1
978-1-912364-22-0	English: Spelling, Punctuation and Grammar Book 2
978-1-912364-00-8	English: Practice Papers Book 1 - Multiple Choice
978-1-912364-01-5	English: Practice Papers Book 2 - Multiple Choice
978-1-912364-17-6	Creative Writing Examples

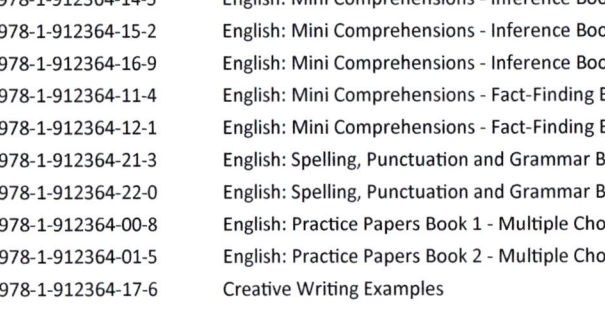

978-1-912364-30-5	Numerical Reasoning: Quick-Fire Book 1
978-1-912364-31-2	Numerical Reasoning: Quick-Fire Book 2
978-1-912364-32-9	Numerical Reasoning: Quick-Fire Book 1 - Multiple Choice
978-1-912364-33-6	Numerical Reasoning: Quick-Fire Book 2 - Multiple Choice
978-1-912364-34-3	Numerical Reasoning: Multi-Part Book 1
978-1-912364-35-0	Numerical Reasoning: Multi-Part Book 2
978-1-912364-36-7	Numerical Reasoning: Multi-Part Book 1 - Multiple Choice
978-1-912364-37-4	Numerical Reasoning: Multi-Part Book 2 - Multiple Choice

978-1-912364-43-5	Mathematics: Mental Arithmetic Book 1
978-1-912364-44-2	Mathematics: Mental Arithmetic Book 2
978-1-912364-45-9	Mathematics: Worded Problems Book 1
978-1-912364-46-6	Mathematics: Worded Problems Book 2
978-1-912364-52-7	Mathematics: Worded Problems Book 3
978-1-912364-47-3	Mathematics: Dictionary Plus
978-1-912364-50-3	Mathematics: Crossword Puzzles Book 1
978-1-912364-51-0	Mathematics: Crossword Puzzles Book 2
978-1-912364-48-0	Mathematics: Practice Papers Book 1 - Multiple Choice
978-1-912364-49-7	Mathematics: Practice Papers Book 2 - Multiple Choice

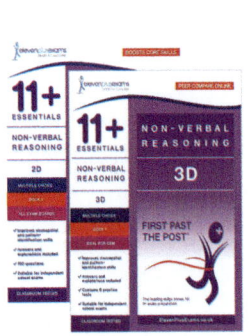

978-1-912364-87-9	Non-Verbal Reasoning: 2D Book 1 - Multiple Choice
978-1-912364-88-6	Non-Verbal Reasoning: 2D Book 2 - Multiple Choice
978-1-912364-85-5	Non-Verbal Reasoning: 3D Book 1 - Multiple Choice
978-1-912364-86-2	Non-Verbal Reasoning: 3D Book 2 - Multiple Choice
978-1-912364-83-1	Non-Verbal Reasoning: Practice Papers Book 1 - Multiple Choice

Contents

Instructions		vi
Test 1	A Little Princess	1
Test 2	Black Beauty	9
Test 3	Heidi	17
Test 4	King Solomon's Mines	25
Test 5	Pollyanna	33
Test 6	The Woman in White	41
Test 7	The Secret Garden	49
Test 8	Tarzan of the Apes	57
Test 9	The Happy Prince	65
Test 10	The Prisoner of Zenda	71
Answers & Explanations		79
Peer-Compare™ access code		inside front cover

This workbook comprises 10 passages of classic fiction, each with 15 comprehension questions and designed to be completed in 12 minutes.

Instructions

Use the method suggested below for working through comprehension papers:

i. Always **read through the passage first**. You should not go straight to the questions. Spend a whole five minutes just reading through the passage.

ii. **Do not skim-read**. Your first reading should be sufficiently thorough so that you have a **good** understanding of the passage and can answer the questions more quickly and accurately. Otherwise, you are unlikely to have sufficient time available.

iii. You should **underline key information** (e.g., names of characters, places, dates, events or other key words that provide an explanation of the subject matter) as this will help you navigate the passage and recall the main points, especially where the question does not provide a line reference. Be careful not to let the underlining slow down your reading or distract you from understanding what you are reading.

iv. Read the questions and then **refer back to the text** in order to find the relevant pieces of information. If you underlined key words and read thoroughly, then you should be able to easily find the relevant parts of the passage that you need in order to answer the questions.

v. There are broadly **four main types of question** as shown in the table opposite. Remember, some questions might be a combination of these different types.

To mark your work, use the 'Answers & Explanations' section at the back of this book. The mark scheme will tell you the correct answer option as well as a short explanation of why this is the case.

For factual content questions, line references are provided to point you towards the location of the answer in the passage.

Where useful, line references are also provided for logical inference and personal judgement questions to indicate where the passage hints at the answer.

Comprehension questions fall into four main types, as shown in the table below:

Type	Where/how to find the answer	Example(s)
Factual content	Specifically stated in the text	Given a text that explains 'When Sophie was 11, she had a terrible accident', you might be asked how old Sophie was at the time of her accident.
Logical inference	Not directly stated in the text but can be inferred from the details given	Given a text that describes the setting as 'cold, snowy and dark', you might be asked what season it is in the story.
Personal judgement	Not directly stated in the text; you must read more deeply into the text to form an opinion	You might be asked about the intentions of the author or how best to describe a character based on what you have read of their speech and actions.
Knowledge of grammar, vocabulary and literary techniques	Not stated in the text at all; you must use your own knowledge to answer the question	Questions may ask about the meaning of a word or ask you to recognise literary techniques, such as alliteration and onomatopoeia. Be careful with vocabulary questions; several answer options may provide a correct definition, but only one will correctly fit the context of the passage.

BLANK PAGE

Test 1

A Little Princess

Total

/15

Read this passage carefully, then answer the questions that follow.

A Little Princess

Frances Hodgson Burnett

1 "Here we are, Sara," said Captain Crewe, making his voice sound as cheerful as possible. Then he lifted her out of the cab and they mounted the steps and rang the bell. Sara often thought afterward that the house was somehow exactly like Miss Minchin. It was respectable and well furnished, but everything in it was ugly; and
5 the very armchairs seemed to have hard bones in them. In the hall everything was hard and polished. The drawing room into which they were ushered was covered by a carpet with a square pattern upon it, the chairs were square, and a heavy marble timepiece stood upon the heavy marble mantel.

As she sat down in one of the stiff mahogany chairs, Sara cast one of her quick
10 looks about her.

"I don't like it, papa," she said. "But then I dare say soldiers—even brave ones—don't really LIKE going into battle."

Captain Crewe laughed at this. He was young and full of fun, and he never tired of hearing Sara's queer speeches.

15 "Oh, little Sara," he said. "What shall I do when I have no one to say solemn things to me? No one else is as solemn as you are."

"But why do solemn things make you laugh so?" inquired Sara.

"Because you are such fun when you say them," he answered, laughing still more. And then suddenly he swept her into his arms and kissed her very hard, stopping
20 laughing all at once and looking almost as if tears had come into his eyes.

It was just then that Miss Minchin entered the room. She was very like her house, Sara felt: tall and dull, and respectable and ugly. She had large, cold, fishy eyes, and a large, cold, fishy smile. It spread itself into a very large smile when she saw Sara and Captain Crewe. She had heard a great many desirable things of the young soldier from
25 the lady who had recommended her school to him. Among other things, she had heard that he was a rich father who was willing to spend a great deal of money on his little daughter.

"It will be a great privilege to have charge of such a beautiful and promising child, Captain Crewe," she said, taking Sara's hand and stroking it. "Lady Meredith has told me of her unusual cleverness. A clever child is a great treasure in an establishment like mine."

Sara stood quietly, with her eyes fixed upon Miss Minchin's face. She was thinking something odd, as usual.

"Why does she say I am a beautiful child?" she was thinking. "I am not beautiful at all. Colonel Grange's little girl, Isobel, is beautiful. She has dimples and rose-colored cheeks, and long hair the colour of gold. I have short black hair and green eyes; besides which, I am a thin child and not fair in the least. I am one of the ugliest children I ever saw. She is beginning by telling a fib."

She was mistaken, however, in thinking she was an ugly child. She was not in the least like Isobel Grange, but she had an odd charm of her own. She was a slim, supple creature, rather tall for her age, and had an intense, attractive little face. Her hair was heavy and quite black and only curled at the tips; her eyes were greenish grey, it is true, but they were big, wonderful eyes with long, black lashes, and though she herself did not like the colour of them, many other people did. Still she was convinced that she was an ugly child, and she was not at all elated by Miss Minchin's flattery.

"I should be telling a fib if I said she was beautiful," she thought; "and I should know I was telling a fib. I believe I am as ugly as she is—in my way. What did she say that for?"

After she had known Miss Minchin longer she learned why she had said it. She discovered that she said the same thing to each parent who brought a child to her school.

Sara stood near her father and listened while he and Miss Minchin talked. She had been brought to the seminary because Lady Meredith's two little girls had been educated there, and Captain Crewe had a great respect for Lady Meredith's experience. Sara was to be what was known as "a parlour boarder," and she was to enjoy great privileges. She was to have a pretty bedroom and sitting room of her own; she was to have a pony and a carriage, and a maid to look after her.

"I am not in the least anxious about her education," Captain Crewe said, with his gay laugh, as he held Sara's hand and patted it. "The difficulty will be to keep her from learning too fast and too much. She is always sitting with her little nose burrowing into books. She doesn't read them, Miss Minchin; she gobbles them up as if she were a wolf instead of a little girl. She is always starving for new books to gobble, and she wants grown-up books— big, fat ones—French and German as well as English— history and biography and poets, and all sorts of things. When she reads too much, make her ride her pony or go and buy a new doll. She ought to play more with dolls."

"Papa," said Sara, "you see, if I went out and bought a new doll every few days I should have more than I could be fond of. Dolls ought to be intimate friends. Emily is going to be my intimate friend."

"Who's Emily?" Miss Minchin inquired.

"Tell her, Sara," Captain Crewe said, smiling.

"She is a doll I haven't got yet," Sara said. "We are going out together to find her. I have called her Emily. She is going to be my friend when papa is gone. I want her to talk to about him."

Miss Minchin's large, fishy smile became very flattering indeed.

"What an original child!" she said. "What a darling little creature!"

"Yes," said Captain Crewe, drawing Sara close. "She is a darling little creature. Take great care of her for me, Miss Minchin."

Please answer these questions. Look at the passage again if you need to.
You should choose the best answer and circle its corresponding letter.

1 Why do you think Captain Crewe is trying to make 'his voice sound as cheerful as possible' (lines 1-2)?

- A He is looking forward to dropping his daughter off at a good school.
- B He wants Sara to think he is happy.
- C He wants to hide the fact that he is angry.
- D He is looking forward to seeing Miss Minchin.
- E He is thinking of something else.

2 Which of the following is the modern-day equivalent of a 'drawing-room' (line 6)?

- A conservatory
- B living room
- C studio
- D study
- E playroom

3 What does the word 'timepiece' refer to in line 8?

- A candlestick
- B barometer
- C sundial
- D hourglass
- E clock

4 Which of these best describes the relationship between Sara and Crewe?

- A loving and intense
- B playful and loving
- C distant and aloof
- D friendly and proper
- E playful and proper

5 What does 'solemn' (line 17) mean?

- A serious
- B funny
- C bizarre
- D confusing
- E unexpected

Please answer these questions. Look at the passage again if you need to.
You should choose the best answer and circle its corresponding letter.

6 Why do you think Captain Crewe stops laughing suddenly and looks 'almost as if tears had come into his eyes'? (line 20)?

- A He is laughing so much it makes him cry.
- B Sara reminds him of his wife.
- C He catches sight of Miss Minchin.
- D He doesn't want to leave Sara.
- E The house reminds him of his past.

7 Which two words best describe both the house and Miss Minchin?

- A proper and old
- B proper and elegant
- C proper and unattractive
- D old and small
- E old and unattractive

8 What is Miss Minchin's profession?

- A housekeeper
- B governess
- C writer
- D headmistress
- E nurse

9 Which of the following pairs of adjectives best describe Captain Crewe?

- A solemn and tall
- B courageous and ugly
- C youthful and kind
- D forthright and generous
- E brave and callous

10 Which of the following are features of Sara's appearance?

- A blonde hair and rosy cheeks
- B blonde hair and blue eyes
- C dark hair and a slender frame
- D a slender frame and blue eyes
- E dark hair and rosy cheeks

Please answer these questions. Look at the passage again if you need to.
You should choose the best answer and circle its corresponding letter.

11 Which of the following is an antonym of 'fib' (line 38)?
- A fabricate
- B falsehood
- C lie
- D story
- E truth

12 Why does Miss Minchin say Sara is beautiful?
- A She wants to persuade Captain Crewe to send Sara to her school.
- B She is being tactful.
- C She is in love with Captain Crewe.
- D She thinks Sara looks like her.
- E She genuinely believes Sara is beautiful.

13 Which of the following is not a benefit given to 'a parlour boarder' (line 55)?
- A a servant
- B a private living room
- C a private room to sleep in
- D their own means of transport
- E a private bathroom

14 What does Captain Crewe jokingly say is a problem with Sara?
- A She plays too much with her dolls.
- B She rides ponies too much.
- C She only reads in French and German instead of English.
- D She reads too much.
- E She reads too little.

15 Who is Emily?
- A Sara's mother
- B Sara's old best friend
- C Sara's maid
- D Sara's old doll
- E Sara's new doll

END OF TEST

BLANK PAGE

Test 2

Black Beauty

Total

/15

Read this passage carefully, then answer the questions that follow.

Black Beauty

Anna Sewell

1   Early in the spring, Lord W—— and part of his family went up to London, and took York with them. I and Ginger and some other horses were left at home for use, and the head groom was left in charge.

       The Lady Harriet, who remained at the hall, was a great invalid, and never went
5 out in the carriage, and the Lady Anne preferred riding on horseback with her brother or cousins. She was a perfect horsewoman, and as gay and gentle as she was beautiful. She chose me for her horse, and named me "Black Auster". I enjoyed these rides very much in the clear cold air, sometimes with Ginger, sometimes with Lizzie. This Lizzie was a bright bay mare, almost thoroughbred, and a great favourite with
10 the gentlemen, on account of her fine action and lively spirit; but Ginger, who knew more of her than I did, told me she was rather nervous.

       There was a gentleman of the name of Blantyre staying at the hall; he always rode Lizzie, and praised her so much that one day Lady Anne ordered the side-saddle to be put on her, and the other saddle on me. When we came to the door the gentleman
15 seemed very uneasy.

       "How is this?" he said. "Are you tired of your good Black Auster?"

       "Oh, no, not at all," she replied, "but I am amiable enough to let you ride him for once, and I will try your charming Lizzie. You must confess that in size and appearance she is far more like a lady's horse than my own favourite."

20   "Do let me advise you not to mount her," he said; "she is a charming creature, but she is too nervous for a lady. I assure you, she is not perfectly safe; let me beg you to have the saddles changed."

       "My dear cousin," said Lady Anne, laughing, "pray do not trouble your good careful head about me. I have been a horsewoman ever since I was a baby, and I have
25 followed the hounds a great many times, though I know you do not approve of ladies hunting; but still that is the fact, and I intend to try this Lizzie that you gentleman are all so fond of; so please help me to mount, like a good friend as you are."

       There was no more to be said; he placed her carefully on the saddle, looked to the bit and curb, gave the reins gently into her hand, and then mounted me. Just as we were moving off a footman came out with a slip of paper and message from the Lady Harriet. "Would they ask this question for her at Dr. Ashley's, and bring the answer?"

The village was about a mile off, and the doctor's house was the last in it. We went along gayly enough till we came to his gate. There was a short drive up to the house between tall evergreens.

Blantyre alighted at the gate, and was going to open it for Lady Anne, but she said, "I will wait for you here, and you can hang Auster's rein on the gate."

He looked at her doubtfully. "I will not be five minutes," he said.

"Oh, do not hurry yourself; Lizzie and I shall not run away from you."

He hung my rein on one of the iron spikes, and was soon hidden among the trees. Lizzie was standing quietly by the side of the road a few paces off, with her back to me. My young mistress was sitting easily with a loose rein, humming a little song. I listened to my rider's footsteps until they reached the house, and heard him knock at the door. There was a meadow on the opposite side of the road, the gate of which stood open; just then some cart horses and several young colts came trotting out in a very disorderly manner, while a boy behind was cracking a great whip. The colts were wild and frolicsome, and one of them bolted across the road and blundered up against Lizzie's hind legs, and whether it was the stupid colt, or the loud cracking of the whip, or both together, I cannot say, but she gave a violent kick, and dashed off into a headlong gallop. It was so sudden that Lady Anne was nearly unseated, but she soon recovered herself. I gave a loud, shrill neigh for help; again and again I neighed, pawing the ground impatiently, and tossing my head to get the rein loose. I had not long to wait. Blantyre came running to the gate; he looked anxiously about, and just caught sight of the flying figure, now far away on the road. In an instant he sprang to the saddle. I needed no whip, no spur, for I was as eager as my rider; he saw it, and giving me a free rein, and leaning a little forward, we dashed after them.

For about a mile and a half the road ran straight, and then bent to the right, after which it divided into two roads. Long before we came to the bend she was out of sight. Which way had she turned? A woman was standing at her garden gate, shading her eyes with her hand, and looking eagerly up the road. Scarcely drawing the rein, Blantyre shouted, "Which way?" "To the right!" cried the woman, pointing with her hand, and away we went up the right-hand road; then for a moment we caught sight of her; another bend and she was hidden again. Several times we caught glimpses, and then lost them. We scarcely seemed to gain ground upon them at all. An old road-mender was standing near a heap of stones, his shovel dropped and his hands

65 raised. As we came near he made a sign to speak. Blantyre drew the rein a little. "To the common, to the common, sir; she has turned off there." I knew this common very well; it was for the most part very uneven ground, covered with heather and dark-green furze bushes, with here and there a scrubby old thorn-tree; there were also open spaces of fine short grass, with ant-hills and mole-turns everywhere; the worst
70 place I ever knew for a headlong gallop.

Please answer these questions. Look at the passage again if you need to.
You should choose the best answer and circle its corresponding letter.

1 What is the name of the narrator?

A   Ginger
B   Lady Harriet
C   Lizzie
D   Black Auster
E   Blantyre

2 Who or what does the word 'invalid' refer to in line 4?

A   the hall
B   Lady Harriet
C   Lady Anne
D   a horse
E   the carriage

3 Which of the following are qualities of Lady Anne?

A   fashionable and dutiful
B   tall and fashionable
C   tender and skilled with horses
D   tender and fashionable
E   tall and skilled with horses

4 What is the problem with Lizzie?

A   She is lazy.
B   She is bad tempered.
C   She is slow.
D   She is too lively.
E   She is skittish.

5 According to Lady Anne, what does Blantyre consider to be unlady-like behaviour?

A   chasing creatures with dogs for sport
B   riding side-saddle
C   having a dog
D   horse riding
E   riding Lizzie

Please answer these questions. Look at the passage again if you need to.
You should choose the best answer and circle its corresponding letter.

6 Why do Lady Anne and Blantyre need to go to the doctor's?
- A to ask him something on behalf of Lady Harriet
- B They are not feeling well.
- C to take him a message from the footman
- D to collect a message
- E to collect some medicine

7 How long does Blantyre think he will have to leave Lady Anne for?
- A a few seconds
- B less than five minutes
- C five minutes
- D just more than five minutes
- E five hours

8 How do we know Lady Anne is feeling happy whilst she is waiting (lines 35-45)?
- A She remains seated on her horse.
- B She laughs out loud.
- C She hums a melody.
- D She whistles a tune.
- E She talks to herself.

9 Which of these is an antonym of 'frolicsome' (line 46)?
- A playful
- B intelligent
- C mischievous
- D frisky
- E sedate

10 Which of the following does the narrator think causes Lizzie to shoot off at a gallop?
- A a violent kick and a loud neigh from the narrator
- B the lash of a whip and a young horse bumping into her
- C a loud neigh from the narrator and a young horse bumping into her
- D the lash of a whip and Lady Anne pulling on her reins
- E Lady Anne pulling on her reins and a violent kick

Please answer these questions. Look at the passage again if you need to.
You should choose the best answer and circle its corresponding letter.

11 Why does Blantyre run to the gate?
- A He hears a dog barking.
- B He hears a horse neighing.
- C He sees Lady Anne galloping off.
- D He hears an altercation.
- E He has accomplished his mission and is anxious to get home.

12 What is meant by the phrase 'to gain ground upon [someone]' in line 63?
- A to overtake someone
- B to knock someone to the ground
- C to draw closer to someone
- D to beat someone in a game
- E to fall far behind someone

13 How many people help Blantyre and Black Auster follow Lady Anne?
- A none
- B one
- C two
- D three
- E four

14 Which of the following is not a reason why the common is a bad place for a headlong gallop?
- A The ground is not flat.
- B There are mole hills.
- C The terrain is very varied.
- D The grass is long.
- E There are prickly plants growing there.

15 Which of the following features make this passage unusual?
- A It is told from the perspective of a horse.
- B It is told from the perspective of a dog.
- C It is told in the third person.
- D It is told in the first person.
- E It does not contain any dialogue.

END OF TEST

Test 3

Heidi

 12 minutes

Total

/15

Read this passage carefully, then answer the questions that follow.

Heidi

Johanna Spyri

1   May had come. Warm sunshine was bathing the whole Alp in glorious light, and having melted the last snow, had brought the first spring flowers to the surface. A merry spring wind was blowing, drying up the damp places in the shadow. High above in the azure heaven the eagle floated peacefully.

5   Heidi and her grandfather were back on the Alp. The child was so happy to be home again that she jumped about among the beloved objects. Here she discovered a new spring bud, and there she watched the gay little gnats and beetles that were swarming in the sun.

   The grandfather was busy in his little shop, and a sound of hammering and sawing
10 could be heard. Heidi had to go and see what the grandfather was making. There before the door stood a neat new chair, while the old man was busy making a second.

   "Oh, I know what they are for," said Heidi gaily. "You are making them for Clara and grandmama. Oh, but we need a third—or do you think that Miss Rottenmeier won't come, perhaps?"

15   "I really don't know," said grandfather: "but it is safer to have a chair for her, if she should come."

   Heidi, thoughtfully looking at the backless chairs, remarked: "Grandfather, I don't think she would sit down on those."

   "Then we must invite her to sit down on the beautiful green lounge of grass,"
20 quietly answered the old man.

   While Heidi was still wondering what the grandfather had meant, Peter arrived, whistling and calling. As usual, Heidi was soon surrounded by the goats, who also seemed happy to be back on the Alp. Peter, angrily pushing the goats aside, marched up to Heidi, thrusting a letter into her hand.

25   "Did you get a letter for me on the pasture?" Heidi said, astonished.

   "No."

   "Where did it come from?"

   "From my bag."

The letter had been given to Peter the previous evening; putting it in his lunch-bag, the boy had forgotten it there till he opened the bag for his dinner. Heidi immediately recognized Clara's handwriting, and bounding over to her grandfather, exclaimed: "A letter has come from Clara. Wouldn't you like me to read it to you, grandfather?"

Heidi immediately read to her two listeners, as follows:—

Dear Heidi:—

We are all packed up and shall travel in two or three days. Papa is leaving, too, but not with us, for he has to go to Paris first. The dear doctor visits us now every day, and as soon as he opens the door, he calls, 'Away to the Alp!' for he can hardly wait for us to go. If you only knew how he enjoyed being with you last fall! He came nearly every day this winter to tell us all about you and the grandfather and the mountains and the flowers he saw. He said that it was so quiet in the pure, delicious air, away from towns and streets, that everybody has to get well there. He is much better himself since his visit, and seems younger and happier. Oh, how I look forward to it all! The doctor's advice is, that I shall go to Ragatz first for about six weeks, then I can go to live in the village, and from there I shall come to see you every fine day. Grandmama, who is coming with me, is looking forward to the trip too. But just think, Miss Rottenmeier does not want to go. When grandmama urges her, she always declines politely. I think Sebastian must have given her such a terrible description of the high rocks and fearful abysses, that she is afraid. I think he told her that it was not safe for anybody, and that only goats could climb such dreadful heights. She used to be so eager to go to Switzerland, but now neither Tinette nor she wants to take the risk. I can hardly wait to see you again!

Good-bye, dear Heidi, with much love from grandmama,

I am your true friend, Clara.

When Peter heard this, he swung his rod to right and left. Furiously driving the goats before him, he bounded down the hill.

Heidi visited the grandmother next day, for she had to tell her the good news. Sitting up in her corner, the old woman was spinning as usual. Her face looked sad, for Peter had already announced the near visit of Heidi's friends, and she dreaded the result.

After having poured out her full heart, Heidi looked at the old woman. "What is it, grandmother?" said the child. "Are you not glad?"

"Oh yes, Heidi, I am glad, because you are happy."

"But, grandmother, you seem anxious. Do you still think Miss Rottenmeier is coming?"

"Oh no, it is nothing. Give me your hand, for I want to be sure that you are still here. I suppose it will be for the best, even if I shall not live to see the day!"

"Oh, but then I would not care about this coming," said the child.

The grandmother had hardly slept all night for thinking of Clara's coming. Would they take Heidi away from her, now that she was well and strong? But for the sake of the child she resolved to be brave.

"Heidi," she said, "please read me the song that begins with 'God will see to it.'"

Heidi immediately did as she was told; she knew nearly all the grandmother's favourite hymns by now and always found them quickly.

"That does me good, child," the old woman said. Already the expression of her face seemed happier and less troubled. "Please read it a few times over, child," she entreated.

Thus evening came, and when Heidi wandered homewards, one twinkling star after another appeared in the sky. Heidi stood still every few minutes, looking up to the firmament in wonder. When she arrived home, her grandfather also was looking up to the stars, murmuring to himself: "What a wonderful month!—one day clearer than the other. The herbs will be fine and strong this year."

The blossom month had passed, and June, with the long, long days, had come. Quantities of flowers were blooming everywhere, filling the air with perfume.

Please answer these questions. Look at the passage again if you need to.
You should choose the best answer and circle its corresponding letter.

1 Which of the following implies that the passage takes place in the spring?

- A snow and blue skies
- B blue skies and emerging flowers
- C blue skies and singing birds
- D singing birds and lambs
- E emerging flowers and snow

2 Which of the following is not one of the 'beloved objects' (line 6) that Heidi has missed whilst away?

- A a gnat
- B an eagle
- C a beetle
- D a flower
- E the sunshine

3 What is Heidi's grandfather doing in his shop?

- A plumbing
- B decorating
- C selling furniture
- D repairing furniture
- E carpentry

4 What does Heidi's grandfather mean when he says 'we must invite her to sit down on the beautiful green lounge of grass' (line 19)?

- A She must sit on the floor of the house.
- B She must sit on the floor outside.
- C She must sit on a green rug.
- D She must stay outside and cannot come into the house.
- E She must sit on a green chair.

5 Who is Peter whistling to?

- A his goats
- B Heidi
- C Heidi's grandfather
- D his lambs
- E the eagle

Please answer these questions. Look at the passage again if you need to.
You should choose the best answer and circle its corresponding letter.

6 How does Heidi know the letter comes from Clara?

- A Peter tells her so.
- B She knows the penmanship.
- C She was expecting a letter from Clara.
- D She recognises the foreign stamp.
- E She doesn't know until she reads Clara's name at the end of the letter.

7 Who are Heidi's 'two listeners' (line 33)?

- A Heidi's grandmother and grandfather
- B Heidi's grandmother and Peter
- C Heidi's grandmother and the goats
- D Heidi's grandfather and Peter
- E Heidi's grandfather and the goats

8 When did Heidi spend time with her friend Clara's doctor?

- A two or three days ago
- B last year
- C last spring
- D last autumn
- E last winter

9 Why is Clara coming to stay with Heidi?

- A to see the sights of Switzerland
- B to meet Peter
- C to learn about nature
- D to help in Heidi's grandfather's shop
- E to improve her health

10 Why does Peter get angry when Heidi reads out Clara's letter?

- A He doesn't like letters.
- B He doesn't like the sound of Heidi's voice.
- C He doesn't like Clara.
- D He is jealous of Heidi's friendship with Clara.
- E He never receives letters from anyone.

Please answer these questions. Look at the passage again if you need to.
You should choose the best answer and circle its corresponding letter.

11 What demonstrates that Heidi's grandmother has poor eyesight?
A   Her eyes are closed.
B   She can't see if Heidi is there.
C   She is wearing glasses.
D   She is spinning.
E   She can't get out of bed.

12 What is Heidi's grandmother worried about?
A   Clara's arrival
B   Heidi's health
C   her own health
D   Clara's health
E   having to be brave

13 Which of the following is the best synonym for 'resolved' (line 70)?
A   renewed
B   wished
C   decided
D   hesitated
E   desired

14 What does 'firmament' (line 79) mean?
A   moon
B   herbs
C   darkness
D   heavens
E   clouds

15 Who is the protagonist of this text?
A   Clara
B   the grandmother
C   Heidi
D   Peter
E   the grandfather

END OF TEST

BLANK PAGE

Test 4

King Solomon's Mines

Total

/15

Read this passage carefully, then answer the questions that follow.

King Solomon's Mines

H. Rider Haggard

1   Let the reader picture to himself the hall of the vastest cathedral he ever stood in, windowless indeed, but dimly lighted from above, presumably by shafts connected with the outer air and driven in the roof, which arched away a hundred feet above our heads, and he will get some idea of the size of the enormous cave in which we found
5   ourselves, with the difference that this cathedral designed by nature was loftier and wider than any built by man. But its stupendous size was the least of the wonders of the place, for running in rows adown its length were gigantic pillars of what looked like ice, but were, in reality, huge stalactites. It is impossible for me to convey any idea of the overpowering beauty and grandeur of these pillars of white spar, some of which
10 were not less than twenty feet in diameter at the base, and sprang up in lofty and yet delicate beauty sheer to the distant roof. Others again were in process of formation. On the rock floor there was in these cases what looked, Sir Henry said, exactly like a broken column in an old Grecian temple, whilst high above, depending from the roof, the point of a huge icicle could be dimly seen.

15 Even as we gazed we could hear the process going on, for presently with a tiny splash a drop of water would fall from the far-off icicle on to the column below. On some columns the drops only fell once in two or three minutes, and in these cases it would be an interesting calculation to discover how long, at that rate of dripping, it would take to form a pillar, say eighty feet by ten in diameter. That the process, in at
20 least one instance, was incalculably slow, the following example will suffice to show. Cut on one of these pillars we discovered the crude likeness of a mummy, by the head of which sat what appeared to be the figure of an Egyptian god, doubtless the handiwork of some old-world labourer in the mine. This work of art was executed at the natural height at which an idle fellow, be he Phoenician workman or British cad, is
25 in the habit of trying to immortalise himself at the expense of nature's masterpieces, namely, about five feet from the ground. Yet at the time that we saw it, which *must* have been nearly three thousand years after the date of the execution of the carving, the column was only eight feet high, and was still in process of formation, which gives a rate of growth of a foot to a thousand years, or an inch and a fraction to a century.
30 This we knew because, as we were standing by it, we heard a drop of water fall.

Sometimes the stalagmites took strange forms, presumably where the dropping of the water had not always been on the same spot. Thus, one huge mass, which must have weighed a hundred tons or so, was in the shape of a pulpit, beautifully fretted over outside with a design that looked like lace. Others resembled strange beasts, and on the sides of the cave were fanlike ivory tracings, such as the frost leaves upon a pane.

Out of the vast main aisle there opened here and there smaller caves, exactly, Sir Henry said, as chapels open out of great cathedrals. Some were large, but one or two—and this is a wonderful instance of how nature carries out her handiwork by the same unvarying laws, utterly irrespective of size—were tiny. One little nook, for instance, was no larger than an unusually big doll's house, and yet it might have been a model for the whole place, for the water dropped, tiny icicles hung, and spar columns were forming in just the same way.

We had not, however, enough time to examine this beautiful cavern so thoroughly as we should have liked, since unfortunately, Gagool seemed to be indifferent as to stalactites, and only anxious to get her business over. This annoyed me the more, as I was anxious to discover by what system the light was admitted into the cave, and whether it was by the hand of man or by that of nature that this was done; also if the place had been used in any way in ancient times, as seemed probable. However, we consoled ourselves with the idea that we would investigate it thoroughly on our way back, and followed on the heels of our uncanny guide.

On she led us, straight to the top of the vast and silent cave, where we found another doorway, not arched as the first was, but square at the top, like the doorways of Egyptian temples.

"Are ye prepared to enter the Place of Death?" asked Gagool, evidently with a view to making us feel uncomfortable.

"Lead on, Macduff," said Good solemnly, trying to look as though he was not at all alarmed, as indeed we all did except Foulata, who caught Good by the arm for protection.

"This is getting rather ghastly," said Sir Henry, peeping into the dark passageway. "Come on, Quatermain—*seniores priores*. We mustn't keep the old lady waiting!" and he politely made way for me to lead the van, for which inwardly I did not bless him.

Tap, tap, went old Gagool's stick down the passage, as she trotted along, chuckling hideously; and still overcome by some unaccountable presentiment of evil, I hung back. "Come, get on, old fellow," said Good, "or we shall lose our fair guide."

Thus adjured, I started down the passage, and after about twenty paces found myself in a gloomy apartment some forty feet long, by thirty broad, and thirty high, which in some past age evidently had been hollowed out of the mountain. This apartment was not nearly so well lighted as the vast stalactite ante-cave, and at the first glance all I could discern was a massive stone table running down its length, with a colossal white figure at its head, and life-sized white figures all round it. Next I discovered a brown thing, seated on the table in the centre, and in another moment my eyes grew accustomed to the light, and I saw what these things were, and was tailing out of the place as hard as my legs could carry me.

Please answer these questions. Look at the passage again if you need to.
You should choose the best answer and circle its corresponding letter.

1 Who is the narrator addressing at the start of the passage?

- A   himself
- B   the reader
- C   Sir Henry
- D   Gagool
- E   Good

2 Where is the narrator?

- A   in a cathedral
- B   in a church
- C   in a cave
- D   in a cell
- E   in a Greek temple

3 How does the narrator feel about the place that he finds himself in?

- A   curious and in awe
- B   curious and suspicious
- C   in shock
- D   suspicious and frightened
- E   frightened and curious

4 What does 'lofty' (line 10) mean?

- A   stunted
- B   soaring
- C   bold
- D   dusty
- E   wet

5 What does the picture engraved on one of the pillars look like?

- A   a Greek deity and an embalmed body
- B   an Egyptian cat and an Egyptian god
- C   an Egyptian cat and an embalmed body
- D   an Egyptian hieroglyph and an Egyptian deity
- E   an Egyptian deity and an embalmed body

Please answer these questions. Look at the passage again if you need to.
You should choose the best answer and circle its corresponding letter.

6 By how much does the narrator estimate that the stalagmites would grow in three hundred years?
- A just over three inches
- B just under three inches
- C just over two inches
- D just under an inch
- E around one foot

7 What are some of the shapes made by the stalagmites said to resemble?
- A a preaching platform and a Roman god
- B frosted leaves and frightening animals
- C a Roman god and frosted leaves
- D frightening animals and a preaching platform
- E a forest and a preaching platform

8 Which of the following means the same as 'irrespective of' (line 40)?
- A concerning
- B regardless of
- C playing heed to
- D paying attention to
- E suspicious of

9 Which of the following best describes Gagool?
- A old and wise
- B wise and devious
- C solemn and thoughtful
- D creepy and youthful
- E strange and malicious

10 Which of these is an antonym of 'indifferent' (line 45)?
- A uncaring
- B irresponsible
- C concerned
- D detached
- E prejudiced

Please answer these questions. Look at the passage again if you need to.
You should choose the best answer and circle its corresponding letter.

11 Which of the following does the narrator want more time to investigate?
- A who had once lived in the cave and where the light was coming from
- B how the light was getting into the cave and whether it had been used long ago
- C how long it took to form a stalagmite
- D how the light was getting into the cave
- E how many smaller caves there were

12 According to the text, which of the following is a feature of Egyptian temples?
- A arched doorways
- B round doorways
- C square pillars
- D square doorways
- E large windows

13 After Gagool, who enters the passageway first?
- A Sir Henry
- B Good
- C Foulata
- D the narrator
- E Good and Foulata together

14 What is the meaning of the Latin phrase *'seniores priores'* in line 61?
- A elders last
- B men first
- C elders first
- D men get priority
- E go ahead

15 What genre does this extract most likely to belong to?
- A horror
- B romance
- C autobiography
- D adventure
- E war

END OF TEST

BLANK PAGE

Test 5

Pollyanna

 12 minutes

Total

/15

Read this passage carefully, then answer the questions that follow.

Pollyanna

Eleanor H. Porter

1   The room contained a small bed, neatly made, two straight-backed chairs, a washstand, a bureau – without any mirror – and a small table. There were no drapery curtains at the dormer windows, no pictures on the wall. All day the sun had been pouring down upon the roof, and the little room was like an oven for heat. As there
5   were no screens, the windows had not been raised. A big fly was buzzing angrily at one of them now, up and down, up and down, trying to get out. Miss Polly killed the fly, swept it through the window (raising the sash an inch for the purpose), straightened a chair, frowned again, and left the room.

"Nancy," she said a few minutes later, at the kitchen door, "I found a fly up-stairs in
10 Miss Pollyanna's room. The window must have been raised at some time. I have ordered screens, but until they come I shall expect you to see that the windows remain closed. My niece will arrive to-morrow at four o'clock. I desire you to meet her at the station. Timothy will take the open buggy and drive you over. The telegram says 'light hair, red-checked gingham dress, and straw hat.' That is all I know, but I think it
15 is sufficient for your purpose."

"Yes, ma'am; but—you—"

Miss Polly evidently read the pause aright, for she frowned and said crisply:

"No, I shall not go. It is not necessary that I should, I think. That is all." And she turned away—Miss Polly's arrangements for the comfort of her niece, Pollyanna,
20 were complete. In the kitchen, Nancy sent her flatiron with a vicious dig across the dish-towel she was ironing.

"'Light hair, red-checked gingham dress, and straw hat'—all she knows, indeed! Well, I'd be ashamed ter own it up, that I would, I would—and her my onliest niece what was a-comin' from 'way across the continent!"

25 Promptly at twenty minutes to four the next afternoon Timothy and Nancy drove off in the open buggy to meet the expected guest. Timothy was Old Tom's son. It was sometimes said in the town that if Old Tom was Miss Polly's right-hand man, Timothy was her left.

Timothy was a good-natured youth, and a good-looking one, as well. Short as had been Nancy's stay at the house, the two were already good friends. To-day, however, Nancy was too full of her mission to be her usual talkative self; and almost in silence she took the drive to the station and alighted to wait for the train.

Over and over in her mind she was saying it "light hair, red-checked dress, straw hat." Over and over again she was wondering just what sort of child this Pollyanna was, anyway.

"I hope for her sake she's quiet and sensible, and don't drop knives nor bang doors," she sighed to Timothy, who had sauntered up to her.

"Well, if she ain't, nobody knows what'll become of the rest of us," grinned Timothy. "Imagine Miss Polly and a NOISY kid! Gorry! there goes the whistle now!"

"Oh, Timothy, I—I think it was mean ter send me," chattered the suddenly frightened Nancy, as she turned and hurried to a point where she could best watch the passengers alight at the little station.

It was not long before Nancy saw her—the slender little girl in the red-checked gingham with two fat braids of flaxen hair hanging down her back. Beneath the straw hat, an eager, freckled little face turned right and left, plainly searching for some one.

Nancy knew the child at once, but not for some time could she control her shaking knees sufficiently to go to her. The little girl was standing quite by herself when Nancy finally did approach her.

"Are you Miss—Pollyanna?" she faltered. The next moment she found herself half smothered in the clasp of two gingham-clad arms.

"Oh, I'm so glad, GLAD, GLAD to see you," cried an eager voice in her ear. "Of course I'm Pollyanna, and I'm so glad you came to meet me! I hoped you would."

"You—you did?" stammered Nancy, vaguely wondering how Pollyanna could possibly have known her—and wanted her. "You—you did?" she repeated, trying to straighten her hat.

"Oh, yes; and I've been wondering all the way here what you looked like," cried the little girl, dancing on her toes, and sweeping the embarrassed Nancy from head to foot, with her eyes. "And now I know, and I'm glad you look just like you do look."

Nancy was relieved just then to have Timothy come up. Pollyanna's words had been most confusing.

"This is Timothy. Maybe you have a trunk," she stammered.

"Yes, I have," nodded Pollyanna, importantly. "I've got a brand-new one. The Ladies'

Aid bought it for me—and wasn't it lovely of them, when they wanted the carpet so? Of course I don't know how much red carpet a trunk could buy, but it ought to buy some, anyhow—much as half an aisle, don't you think? I've got a little thing here in my bag that Mr. Gray said was a check, and that I must give it to you before I could get my trunk. Mr. Gray is Mrs. Gray's husband. They're cousins of Deacon Carr's wife. I came East with them, and they're lovely! And—there, here 'tis," she finished, producing the check after much fumbling in the bag she carried.

Nancy drew a long breath. Instinctively she felt that some one had to draw one – after that speech. Then she stole a glance at Timothy. Timothy's eyes were studiously turned away.

The three were off at last, with Pollyanna's trunk in behind, and Pollyanna herself snugly ensconced between Nancy and Timothy. During the whole process of getting started, the little girl had kept up an uninterrupted stream of comments and questions, until the somewhat dazed Nancy found herself quite out of breath trying to keep up with her.

Please answer these questions. Look at the passage again if you need to.
You should choose the best answer and circle its corresponding letter.

1 What can be told about Miss Polly's character from the way in which she has furnished Pollyanna's room?

- A She is envious.
- B She is kind.
- C She is thrifty.
- D She is sensitive.
- E She is generous.

2 What colour is Pollyanna's hair?

- A blonde
- B auburn
- C chestnut
- D brown
- E black

3 Which of the following is a synonym of 'sufficient' (line 15)?

- A insufficient
- B significant
- C lacking
- D meagre
- E enough

4 Which word in the following line is an adverb?

'she frowned and said crisply' (line 17)

- A she
- B crisply
- C said
- D frowned
- E for

5 Why does Nancy send 'her flatiron with a vicious dig across the dish-towel she was ironing' (line 20-21)?

- A She hates doing the ironing.
- B She objects to Miss Polly's uncaring attitude towards Pollyanna.
- C She woke up in a bad mood.
- D She is tired.
- E She doesn't like being told what to do my Miss Polly.

Please answer these questions. Look at the passage again if you need to.
You should choose the best answer and circle its corresponding letter.

6 What do we learn about Old Tom and Timothy from the phrase 'if Old Tom was Miss Polly's right-hand man, Timothy was her left' (lines 27-28)?
A Timothy is Old Tom and Miss Polly's son.
B Old Tom and Timothy are both in love with Miss Polly.
C Timothy and Old Tom are Miss Polly's employees.
D Old Tom and Timothy are both important assistants to Miss Polly.
E Old Tom and Timothy are handy men.

7 Why does Nancy hope that Pollyanna will be 'quiet and sensible' (line 36)?
A so that she will fit well in Miss Polly's household
B so that she will annoy Miss Polly
C so that she will do well at school
D so that she will get on well with Nancy and Timothy
E so that she will be good company for Old Tom

8 Which of the following is an antonym of 'sauntered' (line 37)?
A jumped
B ambled
C strolled
D walked
E rushed

9 What type of word is 'Gorry' (line 39)?
A a common noun
B a verb
C an utterance
D a proper noun
E an exclamation

10 Aside from her physical description, how else does Nancy identify Pollyanna?
A Pollyanna is clearly looking for somebody.
B Pollyanna is the only child on the platform.
C Pollyanna closely resembles Miss Polly.
D Pollyanna recognises Nancy.
E Pollyanna has lots of luggage.

Please answer these questions. Look at the passage again if you need to.
You should choose the best answer and circle its corresponding letter.

11 Which of the following best describe Pollyanna?
- A   enthusiastic and devious
- B   chatty and devious
- C   enthusiastic and chatty
- D   devious and aloof
- E   aloof and pessimistic

12 Which of the following best characterises the sentence: 'Instinctively she felt that someone had to draw one—after that speech' (lines 70-71)?
- A   factual
- B   amusing
- C   shocking
- D   descriptive
- E   informative

13 What does 'ensconced' (line 74) mean?
- A   forgotten
- B   displaced
- C   settled
- D   squashed
- E   neglected

14 What causes Nancy to feel 'somewhat dazed' (line 76)?
- A   She is exhausted after obeying all of Miss Polly's orders.
- B   She suddenly has a dizzy turn.
- C   She suffers from asthma.
- D   She is stunned by Pollyanna's energy.
- E   She has been doing too much housework.

15 What genre does this extract most likely belong to?
- A   children's fiction
- B   romance
- C   adventure
- D   crime
- E   non-fiction

END OF TEST

BLANK PAGE

Test 6

The Woman in White

Total

/15

Read this passage carefully, then answer the questions that follow.

The Woman in White

Wilkie Collins

1   The heat had been painfully oppressive all day, and it was now a close and sultry night.

My mother and sister had spoken so many last words, and had begged me to wait another five minutes so many times, that it was nearly midnight when the servant
5   locked the garden-gate behind me. I walked forward a few paces on the shortest way back to London, then stopped and hesitated.

The moon was full and broad in the dark blue starless sky, and the broken ground of the heath looked wild enough in the mysterious light to be hundreds of miles away from the great city that lay beneath it. The idea of descending any sooner than I could
10 help into the heat and gloom of London repelled me. The prospect of going to bed in my airless chambers, and the prospect of gradual suffocation, seemed, in my present restless frame of mind and body, to be one and the same thing. I determined to stroll home in the purer air by the most roundabout way I could take; to follow the white winding paths across the lonely heath; and to approach London through its most open
15 suburb by striking into the Finchley Road, and so getting back, in the cool of the new morning, by the western side of the Regent's Park.

I wound my way down slowly over the heath, enjoying the divine stillness of the scene, and admiring the soft alternations of light and shade as they followed each other over the broken ground on every side of me. So long as I was proceeding
20 through this first and prettiest part of my night walk my mind remained passively open to the impressions produced by the view; and I thought but little on any subject— indeed, so far as my own sensations were concerned, I can hardly say that I thought at all.

But when I had left the heath and had turned into the by-road, where there was
25 less to see, the ideas naturally engendered by the approaching change in my habits and occupations gradually drew more and more of my attention exclusively to themselves. By the time I had arrived at the end of the road I had become completely absorbed in my own fanciful visions of Limmeridge House, of Mr. Fairlie, and of the two ladies whose practice in the art of water-colour painting I was so soon to
30 superintend.

I had now arrived at that particular point of my walk where four roads met—the road to Hampstead, along which I had returned, the road to Finchley, the road to West End, and the road back to London. I had mechanically turned in this latter direction, and was strolling along the lonely high-road—idly wondering, I remember, what the Cumberland young ladies would look like—when, in one moment, every drop of blood in my body was brought to a stop by the touch of a hand laid lightly and suddenly on my shoulder from behind me.

I turned on the instant, with my fingers tightening round the handle of my stick.

There, in the middle of the broad bright high-road—there, as if it had that moment sprung out of the earth or dropped from the heaven—stood the figure of a solitary Woman, dressed from head to foot in white garments, her face bent in grave inquiry on mine, her hand pointing to the dark cloud over London, as I faced her.

I was far too startled by the suddenness with which this extraordinary apparition stood before me, in the dead of night and in that lonely place, to ask what she wanted. The strange woman spoke first.

"Is that the road to London?" she said.

I looked attentively at her, as she put that singular question to me. It was then nearly one o'clock. All I could discern distinctly by the moonlight was a colourless, youthful face, meagre and sharp to look at about the cheeks and chin; large, grave, wistfully attentive eyes; nervous, uncertain lips; and light hair of a pale, brownish-yellow hue. There was nothing wild, nothing immodest in her manner: it was quiet and self-controlled, a little melancholy and a little touched by suspicion; not exactly the manner of a lady, and, at the same time, not the manner of a woman in the humblest rank of life. The voice, little as I had yet heard of it, had something curiously still and mechanical in its tones, and the utterance was remarkably rapid. She held a small bag in her hand: and her dress—bonnet, shawl, and gown all of white—was, so far as I could guess, certainly not composed of very delicate or very expensive materials. Her figure was slight, and rather above the average height—her gait and actions free from the slightest approach to extravagance. This was all that I could observe of her in the dim light and under the perplexingly strange circumstances of our meeting. What sort of a woman she was, and how she came to be out alone in the high-road, an hour after midnight, I altogether failed to guess. The one thing of which I felt certain was, that the grossest of mankind could not have misconstrued her motive in speaking, even at that suspiciously late hour and in that suspiciously lonely place.

"Did you hear me?" she said, still quietly and rapidly, without the least fretfulness or impatience. "I asked if that was the way to London."

"Yes," I replied, "that is the way: it leads to St. John's Wood and the Regent's Park. You must excuse my not answering you before. I was rather startled by your sudden appearance in the road; and I am, even now, quite unable to account for it."

70 "You don't suspect me of doing anything wrong, do you? I have done nothing wrong. I have met with an accident—I am very unfortunate in being here alone so late. Why do you suspect me of doing wrong?"

She spoke with unnecessary earnestness and agitation, and shrank back from me several paces. I did my best to reassure her.

75 "Pray don't suppose that I have any idea of suspecting you," I said, "or any other wish than to be of assistance to you, if I can. I only wondered at your appearance in the road, because it seemed to me to be empty the instant before I saw you."

Please answer these questions. Look at the passage again if you need to.
You should choose the best answer and circle its corresponding letter.

1 At what time of the year does this story take place?

- A   early winter
- B   late winter
- C   summer
- D   spring
- E   autumn

2 What has delayed the narrator's departure at the beginning of the extract?

- A   He needed to eat something before he left.
- B   He forgot his coat.
- C   He lost track of time.
- D   His family didn't want him to go.
- E   He didn't want to say goodbye to his family.

3 Which of the following best describe the weather when the narrator begins his walk?

- A   sunny and stifling
- B   stifling and stormy
- C   stormy and clear
- D   stifling and clear
- E   breezy and sunny

4 How is the narrator feeling at the start of the passage?

- A   relaxed
- B   tense
- C   angry
- D   depressed
- E   ecstatic

5 Which of the following is a synonym of 'divine' (line 17)?

- A   scary
- B   pleasant
- C   exciting
- D   boring
- E   heavenly

Please answer these questions. Look at the passage again if you need to.
You should choose the best answer and circle its corresponding letter.

6 What makes the narrator hardly think at all during his walk on the heath?

A He is concentrating on finding his way in the dark.
B He is worried about being out on his own late at night.
C He is too hungry to think much.
D He is too tired to think much.
E He is too busy admiring his surroundings.

7 What is the 'approaching change in [the narrator's]…occupations' (lines 25-26)?

A He is going to be a headmaster in a boarding school.
B He is going to be an artist.
C He is going to be a private art tutor.
D He is going to work in a hotel.
E He is going to be a footman.

8 Where is the narrator when he feels an unexpected touch on his shoulder?

A Limmeridge House
B the heath
C the road to London
D Cumberland
E a crossroads

9 What is the woman in white doing when she meets the narrator?

A walking on the heath
B talking to herself
C admiring the view
D trying to find the route to her destination
E trying to identify the constellations

10 Which of the following is not a feature of the woman's appearance?

A pale face
B slender build
C short stature
D big eyes
E light coloured clothes

Please answer these questions. Look at the passage again if you need to.
You should choose the best answer and circle its corresponding letter.

11 What impression does the reader form of the woman, from the description of her arrival in lines 39-42?
- A She is mysterious and possibly magical.
- B She is poor and in need of help.
- C She is evil and destined to do harm to the narrator.
- D She is familiar and comforting.
- E She is kind and generous.

12 Why does the woman repeat her question to the narrator?
- A She thought he hadn't understood her question.
- B She hadn't heard his answer.
- C She didn't understand his response.
- D She thought she had spoken too fast.
- E She thought he hadn't heard her question.

13 What type of word is 'fretfulness' (line 65)?
- A an adjective
- B an abstract noun
- C an adverb
- D a proper noun
- E a common noun

14 What does the narrator find most surprising about the woman in white?
- A the way she is dressed
- B the suddenness with which she appeared
- C the harshness of her voice
- D her earnestness
- E how fast she spoke

15 What genre does this passage most likely belong to?
- A autobiography
- B romance
- C comedy
- D mystery
- E non-fiction

END OF TEST

BLANK PAGE

Test 7

The Secret Garden

Total

/15

Read this passage carefully, then answer the questions that follow.

The Secret Garden

Frances Hodgson Burnett

1   The sun shone down for nearly a week on the secret garden. The Secret Garden was what Mary called it when she was thinking of it. She liked the name, and she liked still more the feeling that when its beautiful old walls shut her in no one knew where she was. It seemed almost like being shut out of the world in some fairy place. The few
5   books she had read and liked had been fairy-story books, and she had read of secret gardens in some of the stories. Sometimes people went to sleep in them for a hundred years, which she had thought must be rather stupid. She had no intention of going to sleep, and, in fact, she was becoming wider awake every day which passed at Misselthwaite. She was beginning to like to be out of doors; she no longer hated the
10   wind, but enjoyed it. She could run faster, and longer, and she could skip up to a hundred. The bulbs in the secret garden must have been much astonished. Such nice clear places were made round them that they had all the breathing space they wanted, and really, if Mistress Mary had known it, they began to cheer up under the dark earth and work tremendously. The sun could get at them and warm them, and
15   when the rain came down it could reach them at once, so they began to feel very much alive.

     Mary was an odd, determined little person, and now she had something interesting to be determined about, she was very much absorbed, indeed. She worked and dug and pulled up weeds steadily, only becoming more pleased with her work every hour
20   instead of tiring of it. It seemed to her like a fascinating sort of play. She found many more of the sprouting pale green points than she had ever hoped to find. They seemed to be starting up everywhere and each day she was sure she found tiny new ones, some so tiny that they barely peeped above the earth. There were so many that she remembered what Martha had said about the "snowdrops by the thousands," and
25   about bulbs spreading and making new ones. These had been left to themselves for ten years and perhaps they had spread, like the snowdrops, into thousands. She wondered how long it would be before they showed that they were flowers. Sometimes she stopped digging to look at the garden and try to imagine what it would be like when it was covered with thousands of lovely things in bloom.

30   During that week of sunshine, she became more intimate with Ben Weatherstaff. She surprised him several times by seeming to start up beside him as if she sprang out

of the earth. The truth was that she was afraid that he would pick up his tools and go away if he saw her coming, so she always walked toward him as silently as possible. But, in fact, he did not object to her as strongly as he had at first. Perhaps he was secretly rather flattered by her evident desire for his elderly company. Then, also, she was more civil than she had been. He did not know that when she first saw him she spoke to him as she would have spoken to a servant, and had not known that a cross, sturdy old Yorkshire man was not accustomed to be merely commanded to do things.

"Tha'rt like th' robin," he said to her one morning when he lifted his head and saw her standing by him. "I never knows when I shall see thee or which side tha'll come from."

"He's friends with me now," said Mary.

"That's like him," snapped Ben Weatherstaff. "Makin' up to th' women folk just for vanity an' flightiness. There's nothin' he wouldn't do for th' sake o' showin' off an' flirtin' his tail-feathers. He's as full o' pride as an egg's full o' meat."

He very seldom talked much and sometimes did not even answer Mary's questions except by a grunt, but this morning he said more than usual. He stood up and rested one hobnailed boot on the top of his spade while he looked her over.

"How long has tha' been here?" he jerked out.

"I think it's about a month," she answered.

"Tha's beginnin' to do Misselthwaite credit," he said. "Tha's a bit fatter than tha' was an' tha's not quite so yeller. Tha' looked like a young plucked crow when tha' first came into this garden. Thinks I to myself I never set eyes on an uglier, sourer faced young 'un."

Mary was not vain and as she had never thought much of her looks she was not greatly disturbed.

"I know I'm fatter," she said. "My stockings are getting tighter. They used to make wrinkles. There's the robin, Ben Weatherstaff."

There, indeed, was the robin, and she thought he looked nicer than ever. His red waistcoat was as glossy as satin and he flirted his wings and tail and tilted his head and hopped about with all sorts of lively graces. He seemed determined to make Ben Weatherstaff admire him. But Ben was sarcastic.

"Aye, there tha' art!" he said. "Tha' can put up with me for a bit sometimes when tha's got no one better. Tha's been reddinin' up thy waistcoat an' polishin' thy feathers this two weeks. I know what tha's up to. Tha's courtin' some bold young madam somewhere, tellin' thy lies to her about bein' th' finest cock robin on Missel Moor an' ready to fight all th' rest of 'em."

"Oh! look at him!" exclaimed Mary.

The robin was evidently in a fascinating, bold mood. He hopped closer and closer and looked at Ben Weatherstaff more and more engagingly. He flew on to the nearest currant bush and tilted his head and sang a little song right at him.

"Tha' thinks tha'll get over me by doin' that," said Ben, wrinkling his face up in such a way that Mary felt sure he was trying not to look pleased. "Tha' thinks no one can stand out against thee—that's what tha' thinks."

The robin spread his wings—Mary could scarcely believe her eyes. He flew right up to the handle of Ben Weatherstaff's spade and alighted on the top of it. Then the old man's face wrinkled itself slowly into a new expression. He stood still as if he were afraid to breathe—as if he would not have stirred for the world, lest his robin should start away.

Please answer these questions. Look at the passage again if you need to.
You should choose the best answer and circle its corresponding letter.

1 How long does the weather stay fine?

- A just over 24 hours
- B just under 24 hours
- C for a week
- D just over seven days
- E just under seven days

2 Why does Mary like to spend time in 'The Secret Garden'?

- A She dislikes spending time indoors.
- B She loves gardening.
- C No one can find her there.
- D She can sleep peacefully there.
- E She hopes one day she will see fairies.

3 What did Mary particularly dislike about being outdoors when she first arrived at Misselthwaite?

- A getting cold
- B getting wet
- C the garden
- D the wind
- E the robin

4 Which of the following indicate that Mary's fitness is improving?

- A She can stay outdoors for longer.
- B She now enjoys the wind.
- C She has better stamina.
- D She likes being outdoors now.
- E She can win a running race.

5 What literary technique is used to describe the bulbs in lines 11-16?

- A alliteration
- B personification
- C repetition
- D onomatopoeia
- E hyperbole

Please answer these questions. Look at the passage again if you need to.
You should choose the best answer and circle its corresponding letter.

6 How many different word classes are used in the following sentence?
'Mary was an odd, determined little person...' (line 17)
- A one
- B two
- C three
- D four
- E none

7 What are the 'sprouting pale green points' (line 21)?
- A shoots coming up from the bulbs
- B weeds
- C nettles
- D beans beginning to grow
- E peas beginning to grow

8 Which of the following accurately describes the relationship between Ben and Mary?
- A Ben dislikes Mary and tries to avoid her.
- B They have recently grown close and friendlier with each other.
- C Mary treats Ben as her servant and is rude to him.
- D They have always been the best of friends.
- E Mary dislikes Ben and tries to annoy him.

9 What is Ben Weatherstaff's profession?
- A a gardener
- B a builder
- C a landscape designer
- D a scarecrow
- E an artist

10 In what way does Ben think Mary is similar to the robin?
- A She wears red waistcoats.
- B She is small.
- C She likes singing.
- D She has a lot of pride.
- E He never knows when to expect her.

Please answer these questions. Look at the passage again if you need to.
You should choose the best answer and circle its corresponding letter.

11 Which of the following best describe the robin's character?

- A   plucky and cheeky
- B   gallant and gentle
- C   excitable and stupid
- D   secretive and aloof
- E   bold and aggressive

12 Why does Ben think the robin is behaving in such a lively way?

- A   He is trying to make friends with Ben.
- B   He is wooing a mate.
- C   He is trying to scare Ben away.
- D   He is trying to make friends with Mary.
- E   He is building a nest.

13 What does the robin do in an attempt to attract Ben's attention?

- A   He tilts his head at him and pecks him.
- B   He looks at him intently and pecks him.
- C   He pecks him and moves closer to him.
- D   He moves closer and sings him a song.
- E   He sings him a song and pecks him.

14 What is the 'new expression' (line 77) on Ben's face?

- A   terror
- B   anger
- C   confusion
- D   happiness
- E   awe

15 Why does the author give Ben a non-standard style of speech?

- A   to make him seem frightening to Mary
- B   to suggest he has a speech impediment
- C   to make it harder to read the story
- D   as a way of indicating where he comes from
- E   as a way of indicating his age

END OF TEST

Test 8

Tarzan of the Apes

 12 minutes

Total

/15

Read this passage carefully, then answer the questions that follow.

Tarzan of the Apes

Edgar Rice Burroughs

1   From a lofty perch Tarzan viewed the village of thatched huts across the intervening plantation. He saw that at one point the forest touched the village, and to this spot he made his way, lured by a fever of curiosity to behold animals of his own kind, and to learn more of their ways and view the strange lairs in which they lived.

5   His savage life among the fierce wild brutes of the jungle left no opening for any thought that these could be aught else than enemies. Similarity of form led him into no erroneous conception of the welcome that would be accorded him should he be discovered by these, the first of his own kind he had ever seen.

Tarzan of the Apes was no sentimentalist. He knew nothing of the brotherhood of
10   man. All things outside his own tribe were his deadly enemies, with the few exceptions of which Tantor, the elephant, was a marked example. And he realized all this without malice or hatred. To kill was the law of the wild world he knew. Few were his primitive pleasures, but the greatest of these was to hunt and kill, and so he accorded to others the right to cherish the same desires as he, even though he himself
15   might be the object of their hunt.

His strange life had left him neither morose nor bloodthirsty. That he joyed in killing, and that he killed with a joyous laugh upon his handsome lips betokened no innate cruelty. He killed for food most often, but, being a man, he sometimes killed for pleasure, a thing which no other animal does; for it has remained for man alone
20   among all creatures to kill senselessly and wantonly for the mere pleasure of inflicting suffering and death. And when he killed for revenge, or in self-defense, he did that also without hysteria, for it was a very businesslike proceeding which admitted of no levity. So it was that now, as he cautiously approached the village of Mbonga, he was quite prepared either to kill or be killed should he be discovered. He proceeded with
25   unwonted stealth, for Kulonga had taught him great respect for the little sharp splinters of wood which dealt death so swiftly and unerringly.

At length he came to a great tree, heavy laden with thick foliage and loaded with pendant loops of giant creepers. From this almost impenetrable bower above the village he crouched, looking down upon the scene below him, wondering over every
30   feature of this new, strange life.

There were naked children running and playing in the village street. There were women grinding dried plantain in crude stone mortars, while others were fashioning cakes from the powdered flour. Out in the fields he could see still other women hoeing, weeding, or gathering. All wore strange protruding girdles of dried grass about their hips and many were loaded with brass and copper anklets, armlets and bracelets. Around many a dusky neck hung curiously coiled strands of wire, while several were further ornamented by huge nose rings.

Tarzan of the Apes looked with growing wonder at these strange creatures. Dozing in the shade he saw several men, while at the extreme outskirts of the clearing he occasionally caught glimpses of armed warriors apparently guarding the village against surprise from an attacking enemy. He noticed that the women alone worked. Nowhere was there evidence of a man tilling the fields or performing any of the homely duties of the village.

Finally his eyes rested upon a woman directly beneath him. Before her was a small cauldron standing over a low fire and in it bubbled a thick, reddish, tarry mass. On one side of her lay a quantity of wooden arrows the points of which she dipped into the seething substance, then laying them upon a narrow rack of boughs which stood upon her other side.

Tarzan was fascinated. Here was the secret of the terrible destructiveness of The Archer's tiny missiles. He noted the extreme care which the woman took that none of the matter should touch her hands, and once when a particle spattered upon one of her fingers he saw her plunge it into a vessel of water and quickly rub the tiny stain away with a handful of leaves.

Tarzan knew nothing of poison, but his shrewd reasoning told him that it was this deadly stuff that killed, and not the little arrow, which was merely the messenger that carried it into the body of its victim. How he should like to have more of those little death-dealing slivers. If the woman would only leave her work for an instant he could drop down, gather up a handful, and be back in the tree again before she drew three breaths.

As he was trying to think out some plan to distract her attention he heard a wild cry from across the clearing. He looked and saw a black warrior standing beneath the very tree in which he had killed the murderer of Kala an hour before. The fellow was shouting and waving his spear above his head. Now and again he would point to something on the ground before him.

The village was in an uproar instantly. Armed men rushed from the interior of their huts and raced madly across the clearing toward the excited sentry. After them trooped the old men, and the women and children until, in a moment, the village was deserted. Tarzan of the Apes knew that they had found the body of his victim, but that interested him far less than the fact that no one remained in the village to prevent his taking a supply of the arrows which lay below him.

Quickly and noiselessly he dropped to the ground beside the cauldron of poison. For a moment he stood motionless, his quick, bright eyes scanning the interior of the palisade. No one was in sight. His eyes rested upon the open doorway of a nearby hut. He would take a look within, thought Tarzan, and so, cautiously, he approached the low thatched building.

Please answer these questions. Look at the passage again if you need to. You should choose the best answer and circle its corresponding letter.

1 At the start of the passage, why is Tarzan going to the village?
- A to meet some friends
- B to meet some family members
- C to observe and discover more about human beings
- D to escape from the apes
- E to find a new place to live

2 What does the word 'brutes' refer to in line 5?
- A animals
- B monsters
- C human beings
- D ogres
- E demons

3 Which of the following has the opposite meaning to the word 'erroneous' (line 7)?
- A mistaken
- B wrong
- C fantastic
- D important
- E correct

4 Which of the following activities does Tarzan enjoy doing?
- A eating bananas
- B daydreaming
- C killing for revenge
- D climbing trees
- E hunting

5 Which of the following pairs of adjectives best describe Tarzan?
- A cruel and vicious
- B bad tempered and aggressive
- C ugly and weak
- D good-looking and athletic
- E careful and sensible

Please answer these questions. Look at the passage again if you need to.
You should choose the best answer and circle its corresponding letter.

6 Why does Tarzan most often kill his prey?
A   he enjoys it
B   in order to demonstrate his strength
C   it provides him with nourishment
D   in order to defend himself
E   in order to defend members of his tribe

7 Who or what does 'Kulonga' (line 25) refer to ?
A   an ape in Tarzan's tribe
B   Tarzan's mother
C   Tarzan's teacher at school
D   an elephant
E   Tarzan's sweetheart

8 What is Tarzan referring to as 'the little sharp splinters of wood which dealt death so swiftly and unerringly' (lines 25-26)?
A   darts
B   catapults
C   swords
D   spears
E   axes

9 Why is the tree in which Tarzan hides himself described as an 'impenetrable bower' (line 28)?
A   It is too tall for anyone to climb.
B   The branches are too thick to stand on.
C   The branches are too weak to stand on.
D   It is a habitat of dangerous wild animals.
E   Its leaves are so dense that anyone under them is concealed from view.

10 Which of the following duties are the women of the village performing?
A   cleaning out the huts
B   looking at the children
C   guarding the village
D   hunting in the jungle
E   cultivating crops

Please answer these questions. Look at the passage again if you need to.
You should choose the best answer and circle its corresponding letter.

11 What part of the women's bodies is not adorned by ornaments?
- A wrist
- B waist
- C ankle
- D nostrils
- E upper arm

12 How does Tarzan feel when he realises what the woman is creating?
- A excited
- B furious
- C terrified
- D devastated
- E disappointed

13 What causes the village to be 'in an uproar' (line 65) all of a sudden?
- A The men discover the woman is making poisoned arrows.
- B One of the village children goes missing.
- C Another tribe is coming to attack the village.
- D A dangerous elephant is spotted near the village.
- E A dead person is discovered under a tree near the village.

14 Which of the following words means the same as 'motionless' (line 72)?
- A immobile
- B mobile
- C undecided
- D indecisive
- E hesitant

15 What is Tarzan's most unique characteristic?
- A He killed someone.
- B He is handsome.
- C He was raised by apes.
- D He is an ape.
- E He is skilled at hunting.

END OF TEST

BLANK PAGE

Test 9

The Happy Prince

Total

/15

Read this passage carefully, then answer the questions that follow.

The Happy Prince

Oscar Wilde

1   High above the city, on a tall column, stood the statue of the Happy Prince. He was gilded all over with thin leaves of fine gold, for eyes he had two bright sapphires, and a large red ruby glowed on his sword-hilt.

He was very much admired indeed. "He is as beautiful as a weathercock," 5   remarked one of the Town Councillors who wished to gain a reputation for having artistic tastes; "only not quite so useful," he added, fearing lest people should think him unpractical, which he really was not.

"Why can't you be like the Happy Prince?" asked a sensible mother of her little boy who was crying for the moon. "The Happy Prince never dreams of crying for 10 anything."

"I am glad there is someone in the world who is quite happy," muttered a disappointed man as he gazed at the wonderful statue.

"He looks just like an angel," said the Charity Children as they came out of the cathedral in their bright scarlet cloaks and their clean white pinafores.

15 "How do you know?" said the Mathematical Master, "you have never seen one."

"Ah! but we have, in our dreams," answered the children; and the Mathematical Master frowned and looked very severe, for he did not approve of children dreaming.

One night there flew over the city a little Swallow. His friends had gone away to Egypt six weeks before, but he had stayed behind, for he was in love with the most 20 beautiful Reed. He had met her early in the spring as he was flying down the river after a big yellow moth, and had been so attracted by her slender waist that he had stopped to talk to her.

"Shall I love you?" said the Swallow, who liked to come to the point at once, and the Reed made him a low bow. So he flew round and round her, touching the water 25 with his wings, and making silver ripples. This was his courtship, and it lasted all through the summer.

"It is a ridiculous attachment," twittered the other Swallows; "she has no money, and far too many relations," and indeed the river was quite full of Reeds. Then, when the autumn came they all flew away.

After they had gone he felt lonely, and began to tire of his lady-love. "She has no conversation," he said, "and I am afraid that she is a coquette, for she is always flirting with the wind." And certainly, whenever the wind blew, the Reed made the most graceful curtseys. "I admit that she is domestic," he continued, "but I love travelling, and my wife, consequently, should love travelling also."

"Will you come away with me?" he said finally to her; but the Reed shook her head, she was so attached to her home.

"You have been trifling with me," he cried. "I am off to the Pyramids. Good-bye!" and he flew away.

All day long he flew, and at night-time he arrived at the city. "Where shall I put up?" he said; "I hope the town has made preparations." Then he saw the statue on the tall column. "I will put up there," he cried; "it is a fine position, with plenty of fresh air." So he alighted just between the feet of the Happy Prince.

"I have a golden bedroom," he said softly to himself as he looked round, and he prepared to go to sleep; but just as he was putting his head under his wing a large drop of water fell on him. "What a curious thing!" he cried; "there is not a single cloud in the sky, the stars are quite clear and bright, and yet it is raining. The climate in the north of Europe is really dreadful. The Reed used to like the rain, but that was merely her selfishness."

Then another drop fell.

"What is the use of a statue if it cannot keep the rain off?" he said; "I must look for a good chimney-pot," and he determined to fly away. But before he had opened his wings, a third drop fell, and he looked up— Ah! what did he see? The eyes of the Happy Prince were filled with tears, and tears were running down his golden cheeks. His face was so beautiful in the moonlight that the little Swallow was filled with pity.

"Who are you?" he said.

"I am the Happy Prince."

"Why are you weeping then?" asked the Swallow; "you have quite drenched me."

"When I was alive and had a human heart," answered the statue, "I did not know what tears were, for I lived in the Palace of Sans-Souci, where sorrow is not allowed to enter. In the daytime I played with my companions in the garden, and in the evening I led the dance in the Great Hall. Round the garden ran a very lofty wall, but I never cared to ask what lay beyond it, everything about me was so beautiful. My courtiers called me the Happy Prince, and happy indeed I was, if pleasure be happiness. So I lived, and so I died. And now that I am dead they have set me up here so high that I can see all the ugliness and all the misery of my city, and though my heart is made of lead yet I cannot choose but weep."

"What! is he not solid gold?" said the Swallow to himself. He was too polite to make any personal remarks out loud.

"Far away," continued the statue in a low musical voice, "far away in a little street there is a poor house. One of the windows is open, and through it I can see a woman seated at a table. Her face is thin and worn, and she has coarse, red hands, all pricked by the needle, for she is a seamstress. She is embroidering passion-flowers on a satin gown for the loveliest of the Queen's maids-of-honour to wear at the next Court-ball. In a bed in the corner of the room her little boy is lying ill. He has a fever, and is asking for oranges. His mother has nothing to give him but river water, so he is crying. Swallow, Swallow, little Swallow, will you not bring her the ruby out of my sword-hilt? My feet are fastened to this pedestal and I cannot move."

Please answer these questions. Look at the passage again if you need to.
You should choose the best answer and circle its corresponding letter.

1 What are 'sapphires' (line 2)?

A pieces of marble
B jewels
C pebbles
D pieces of coal
E pieces of coral

2 Why does the Town Councillor comment on the statue's appearance?

A He wants people to think he has an appreciation of beauty.
B He wants people to think he is unpractical.
C He wants people to think he created the statue.
D He wants people to think he is sensible.
E He wants people to vote for him in the next council election.

3 Why is a weathercock useful?

A It is beautiful.
B It can predict rainfall.
C It can indicate what time it is.
D It can indicate the level of pressure in the atmosphere.
E It can indicate which direction the wind is coming from.

4 Why does the mother want her son to be more like the Happy Prince?

A Her son is crying.
B Her son is always happy.
C Her son always asks for the impossible.
D Her son is not acting sensibly.
E Her son is too active.

5 What colour are the cloaks of the Charity Children?

A blue
B grey
C pink
D red
E black

Please answer these questions. Look at the passage again if you need to.
You should choose the best answer and circle its corresponding letter.

6 Why does the little Swallow stay behind when his friends fly to Egypt?

A   He had fallen in love with a yellow moth.
B   He has already been there before.
C   He has fallen in love with a plant.
D   He has fallen in love with the wind.
E   He is too tired to fly all the way to Egypt.

7 Why do the Swallow's friends think the object of his love is unsuitable?

A   She is not a bird and is already in love with the wind.
B   She is already in love with the wind and is poor.
C   She is poor and is in love with too many others.
D   She is poor and her family is too large.
E   She can't speak and her family is too large.

8 Which of the following is the best synonym for 'alighted' (line 42)?

A   landed
B   stopped
C   hovered
D   took off
E   lessen

9 What is the meaning of the word 'curious' in line 45?

A   nosey
B   strange
C   inquisitive
D   hilarious
E   brilliant

10 From what we're told in the passage, which country is this story most likely to be set?

A   Egypt
B   Spain
C   China
D   America
E   Germany

Please answer these questions. Look at the passage again if you need to.
You should choose the best answer and circle its corresponding letter.

11 Why is the statue known as 'the Happy Prince'?
- A He is made of precious materials.
- B He has the best viewpoint in the city from the top of the pillar.
- C He did lots of good deeds throughout his lifetime.
- D He had a beautiful wife.
- E He dedicated himself to enjoyment throughout his life.

12 Which of the following best describes the Happy Prince's voice?
- A loud and bellowing
- B soft and harmonious
- C sharp and shrill
- D hearty and jolly
- E husky and mysterious

13 What is the job of the poor woman the Happy Prince wishes to help?
- A cleaner
- B nurse
- C clothes maker
- D washerwoman
- E nanny

14 Why do you think the Happy Prince wants to help poor people?
- A to continue with what he did when he was alive
- B to give the Swallow something to do
- C to impress the people in the town
- D to impress the Swallow
- E to make up for not doing so before

15 Why can't the Happy Prince move?
- A His body is too heavy.
- B He is weeping too much.
- C His feet are bolted to the ground.
- D He does not know how to walk.
- E He does not have feet.

END OF TEST

BLANK PAGE

Test 10

The Prisoner of Zenda

 12 minutes

Total

/15

Read this passage carefully, then answer the questions that follow.

The Prisoner of Zenda

Anthony Hope

1   I took an early luncheon, and, having bidden my kind entertainers farewell, promising to return to them on my way home, I set out to climb the hill that led to the Castle, and thence to the forest of Zenda. Half an hour's leisurely walking brought me to the Castle. It had been a fortress in old days, and the ancient keep was still in good
5   preservation and very imposing. Behind it stood another portion of the original castle, and behind that again, and separated from it by a deep and broad moat, which ran all round the old buildings, was a handsome modern chateau, erected by the last king, and now forming the country residence of the Duke of Strelsau. The old and the new portions were connected by a drawbridge, and this indirect mode of access formed
10   the only passage between the old building and the outer world; but leading to the modern chateau there was a broad and handsome avenue. It was an ideal residence: when Michael desired company, he could dwell in his chateau; if a fit of misanthropy seized him, he had merely to cross the bridge and draw it up after him (it ran on rollers), and nothing short of a regiment and a train of artillery could fetch him out. I
15   went on my way, glad that poor Michael, though he could not have the throne or the princess, had, at least, as fine a residence as any prince in Europe.

     Soon I entered the forest, and walked on for an hour or more in its cool sombre shade. The great trees enlaced with one another over my head, and the sunshine stole through in patches as bright as diamonds, and hardly bigger. I was enchanted
20   with the place, and, finding a felled tree-trunk, propped my back against it, and stretching my legs out gave myself up to undisturbed contemplation of the solemn beauty of the woods and to the comfort of a good cigar. And when the cigar was finished and I had (I suppose) inhaled as much beauty as I could, I went off into the most delightful sleep, regardless of my train to Strelsau and of the fast-waning
25   afternoon. To remember a train in such a spot would have been rank sacrilege. Instead of that, I fell to dreaming that I was married to the Princess Flavia and dwelt in the Castle of Zenda, and beguiled whole days with my love in the glades of the forest—which made a very pleasant dream. In fact, I was just impressing a fervent kiss on the charming lips of the princess, when I heard (and the voice seemed at first a
30   part of the dream) someone exclaim, in rough strident tones.

     "Why, the devil's in it! Shave him, and he'd be the King!"

The idea seemed whimsical enough for a dream: by the sacrifice of my heavy moustache and carefully pointed imperial, I was to be transformed into a monarch! I was about to kiss the princess again, when I arrived (reluctantly) at the conclusion that I was awake.

I opened my eyes, and found two men regarding me with much curiosity. Both wore shooting costumes and carried guns. One was rather short and very stoutly built, with a big bullet-shaped head, a bristly grey moustache, and small pale-blue eyes, a trifle bloodshot. The other was a slender young fellow, of middle height, dark in complexion, and bearing himself with grace and distinction. I set the one down as an old soldier: the other for a gentleman accustomed to move in good society, but not unused to military life either. It turned out afterwards that my guess was a good one.

The elder man approached me, beckoning the younger to follow. He did so, courteously raising his hat. I rose slowly to my feet.

"He's the height, too!" I heard the elder murmur, as he surveyed my six feet two inches of stature. Then, with a cavalier touch of the cap, he addressed me: "May I ask your name?"

"As you have taken the first step in the acquaintance, gentlemen," said I, with a smile, "suppose you give me a lead in the matter of names."

The young man stepped forward with a pleasant smile.

"This," said he, "is Colonel Sapt, and I am called Fritz von Tarlenheim: we are both in the service of the King of Ruritania."

I bowed and, baring my head, answered:

"I am Rudolf Rassendyll. I am a traveller from England; and once for a year or two I held a commission from her Majesty the Queen."

"Then we are all brethren of the sword," answered Tarlenheim, holding out his hand, which I took readily.

"Rassendyll, Rassendyll!" muttered Colonel Sapt; then a gleam of intelligence flitted across his face.

"By Heaven!" he cried, "you're of the Burlesdons?"

"My brother is now Lord Burlesdon," said I.

"Thy head betrayeth thee," he chuckled, pointing to my uncovered poll. "Why, Fritz, you know the story?"

The young man glanced apologetically at me. He felt a delicacy which my sister-in-law would have admired. To put him at his ease, I remarked with a smile:

"Ah! the story is known here as well as among us, it seems."

"Known!" cried Sapt. "If you stay here, the deuce a man in all Ruritania will doubt of it—or a woman either."

I began to feel uncomfortable. Had I realized what a very plainly written pedigree I carried about with me, I should have thought long before I visited Ruritania. However, I was in for it now.

At this moment a ringing voice sounded from the wood behind us:

"Fritz, Fritz! where are you, man?"

Tarlenheim started, and said hastily:

"It's the King!"

Old Sapt chuckled again.

Then a young man jumped out from behind the trunk of a tree and stood beside us. As I looked at him, I uttered an astonished cry; and he, seeing me, drew back in sudden wonder. Saving the hair on my face and a manner of conscious dignity which his position gave him, saving also that he lacked perhaps half an inch—nay, less than that, but still something—of my height, the King of Ruritania might have been Rudolf Rassendyll, and I, Rudolf, the King.

Please answer these questions. Look at the passage again if you need to.
You should choose the best answer and circle its corresponding letter.

1 What is the time of day at the start of the story?

- A daybreak
- B morning
- C mid afternoon
- D late afternoon
- E evening

2 How long does it take for the narrator to reach the Castle?

- A 10 minutes
- B 20 minutes
- C 30 minutes
- D 60 minutes
- E a day

3 What joins the old and new parts of the Castle together?

- A a raisable bridge
- B a tower bridge
- C a wide avenue
- D a forest path
- E a moat

4 Who built the modern chateau?

- A the previous monarch
- B the Duke of Strelsau
- C Michael
- D the narrator
- E Princess Flavia

5 Which of the following is the best antonym for 'sombre' in line 17?

- A depressing
- B gloomy
- C dark
- D bright
- E exciting

Please answer these questions. Look at the passage again if you need to.
You should choose the best answer and circle its corresponding letter.

6 Why does the writer compare sunshine with diamonds in lines 18-19?
- A They are both a similar shape.
- B They both produce light
- C They both produce heat
- D They both have a hard core.
- E They are of a similar brightness.

7 What best describes the situation of the narrator in his dream?
- A He is hunting deer in a forest.
- B He is living in a chateau with his royal wife.
- C He is playing with his children in the Castle.
- D He is walking through a wood with his children.
- E He is living in a chateau with the King.

8 Which of the following is the best synonym for 'whimsical' in line 32?
- A fanciful
- B suitable
- C normal
- D fitting
- E sensible

9 What do the two men who come across the narrator in the forest have in common?
- A They are both old.
- B They are both young.
- C They both know the narrator.
- D They are both sons of the King.
- E They are both in the army.

10 What is the narrator doing when he 'bare[s] [his] head' in line 52?
- A shaving his head
- B taking his hat off
- C shaving his beard off
- D taking his wig off
- E taking his coat off

Please answer these questions. Look at the passage again if you need to.
You should choose the best answer and circle its corresponding letter.

11 Which imaginary country is the story set in?

- A Zenda
- B Strelsau
- C England
- D Ruritania
- E Tarlenheim

12 With regards to the narrator, which of the following is not true?

- A Lord Burlesdon is his sibling.
- B His name is Rudolf.
- C He is in love with Princess Flavia.
- D He is short.
- E He has a lot of facial hair.

13 Why are the narrator and the King so surprised when they see each other?

- A They weren't expecting to meet in such an informal situation.
- B They realise they have the same hairstyle.
- C They realise they are nearly identical to each other.
- D They realise they are related to each other.
- E They realise they are the same height.

14 Who is the main character in this passage?

- A Rudolf Rassendyll
- B Colonel Sapt
- C the King of Ruritania
- D Fritz von Tarlenheim
- E Princess Flavia

15 What genre does this passage most likely belong to?

- A comedy
- B journalism
- C fantasy
- D non-fiction
- E adventure

END OF TEST

BLANK PAGE

FIRST PAST THE POST

Answers & Explanations

English: Comprehensions

Classic Literature

Book 2

Test 1 - A Little Princess, pages 1-8

Question	Answer	Explanation
1	B	Reader's personal judgement required. It becomes clear during the passage that they are visiting a school where Sara will become a boarder, and Captain Crewe is trying to make Sara feel happy about being left there.
2	B	Knowledge of vocabulary required. A drawing room was where guests were entertained or where family members relaxed together at leisure. The closest modern equivalent of this is a living room.
3	E	Knowledge of vocabulary required. 'Timepiece' is a word for a clock. The fact that this 'timepiece' was placed on the mantelpiece is a good hint that it is a clock rather than any of the other time-measuring devices.
4	B	Reader's personal judgement required. Refer to lines 13-14 'He was young and full of fun, and he never tired of hearing Sara's queer speeches' and line 19 'suddenly he swept her into his arms and kissed her very hard' to help form an opinion as to the relationship between Sara and Crewe. Sara also refers to Captain Crewe as 'papa' in line 11. We can infer that Crewe is a loving and playful father.
5	A	Knowledge of vocabulary required. 'Solemn' means formal and dignified, and 'serious' means reflective and humourless. Therefore, the best option is A: serious.
6	D	Reader's personal judgement required. Refer to lines 19-20: '… he swept [Sara] into his arms and kissed her very hard, stopping laughing all at once and looking almost as if tears had come into his eyes.' It can be inferred from these lines that Crewe cares deeply for Sara, and the implication is that he is sad at having to leave her.
7	C	Refer to lines 21-22: '[Miss Minchin] was very like her house, Sara felt: tall and dull, and respectable and ugly'. 'Proper' and 'unattractive' are synonyms for 'respectable' and 'ugly' respectively.
8	D	Refer to lines 24-25: '[Miss Minchin] had heard a great many desirable things of the young soldier from the lady who had recommended her school to him.' As the owner of the school, she would be the headmistress.
9	C	Reader's personal judgement required. In line 13, Captain Crewe is described as 'young and full of fun' and throughout the text he treats Sara with affection and kindness, hugging her and patting her hand, so 'youthful and kind' is the best description.
10	C	Refer to lines 40-42: 'She was a slim, supple creature, rather tall for her age, and had an intense, attractive little face. Her hair was heavy and quite black…'
11	E	Knowledge of vocabulary required. 'Truth' means the quality of being true or a fact, which is the opposite of 'fib'. Therefore, the best option is E: truth.
12	A	Reader's logical inference required. Refer to lines 49-51: 'After [Sara] had known Miss Minchin longer she learned why she had said [that she was beautiful]. She discovered that she said the same thing to each parent who brought a child to her school.' The implication is that Miss Minchin is flattering the children in order to persuade the parents to send them to her school.
13	E	Refer to lines 56-57: '…a pretty bedroom and sitting room of her own…a pony and a carriage, and a maid to look after her.' A bathroom of her own is not mentioned.
14	D	Refer to lines 59-61: 'The difficulty will be to keep her from learning too fast and too much. She is always sitting with her little nose burrowing into books. She doesn't read them, Miss Minchin; she gobbles them up…'
15	E	Refer to line 71: 'She is a doll I haven't got yet…'

Test 2 - Black Beauty, pages 9-16

Question	Answer	Explanation
1	D	Refer to line 7: '[Lady Anne] chose me for her horse, and named me 'Black Auster.'
2	B	Refer to line 4: 'The Lady Harriet, who remained at the hall, was a great invalid…' The word 'invalid' here is an adjective used to describe Lady Harriet.
3	C	Refer to lines 6-7: 'She was a perfect horsewoman, and as gay and gentle as she was beautiful.'
4	E	Refer to lines 20-21: '"Do let me advise you not to mount her," he said; "she is a charming creature, but she is too nervous for a lady."'
5	A	Refer to lines 24-26: 'I have followed the hounds a great many times, though I know you do not approve of ladies hunting…'
6	A	Refer to lines 29-31: 'Just as we were moving off a footman came out with a slip of paper and message from the Lady Harriet. "Would they ask this question for her at Dr. Ashley's, and bring the answer?"'
7	B	Refer to line 37: 'I will not be five minutes…'
8	C	Reader's personal judgement required. Refer to line 41: 'My young mistress was sitting easily with a loose rein, humming a little song.'
9	E	Knowledge of vocabulary required. 'Frolicsome' means playful and lively, and 'sedate' means calm. Therefore, the best option is E: sedate.
10	B	Refer to lines 46-48: '…one of [the colts] bolted across the road and blundered up against Lizzie's hind legs, and whether it was the stupid colt, or the loud cracking of the whip, or both together, I cannot say…'
11	B	Refer to lines 50-52: 'I gave a loud, shrill neigh for help; again and again I neighed… I had not long to wait. Blantyre came running to the gate…'
12	C	Knowledge of vocabulary required. 'To gain ground on someone' means to draw closer to them.
13	C	Refer to lines 58-66. Blantyre asks a woman which way Lady Anne has gone, and a stone cutter volunteers the information without being asked by Blantyre. Therefore, two people help Blantyre and Black Auster follow Lady Anne.
14	D	Refer to lines 67-69: '…it was for the most part very uneven ground, covered with heather and dark-green furze bushes, with here and there a scrubby old thorn-tree; there were also open spaces of fine short grass, with ant-hills and mole-turns everywhere…'
15	A	Reader's personal judgement required. Refer to the passage as a whole to make a decision. The unusual thing about the passage is that it is narrated by a horse.

Test 3 - Heidi, pages 17-24

Question	Answer	Explanation
1	B	Reader's logical inference required. Refer to lines 1-4: 'Warm sunshine…had brought the first spring flowers to the surface… High above in the azure heaven the eagle floated peacefully.'
2	A	Refer to lines 6-8: '…she jumped about among the beloved objects. Here she discovered a new spring bud, and there she watched the gay little gnats and beetles that were swarming in the sun.' The only thing that is not mentioned in this list is an eagle.
3	E	Reader's logical inference required. Refer to lines 9-10: 'The grandfather was busy in his little shop, and a sound of hammering and sawing could be heard.' Heidi's grandfather is construction his own furniture, therefore the best option is E.
4	B	Reader's logical inference required. Refer to the context of the quoted phrase in the passage to help make a decision as to its meaning. Heidi doubts Miss Rottenmeier would sit on a stool, therefore it is likely that her grandfather is suggesting she must sit on the floor instead. He describes the floor as a 'beautiful green lounge of grass' (line 19), therefore the most likely option is B: she must sit on the floor outside.
5	A	Reader's logical inference required. Refer to lines 21-23: '…Peter arrived, whistling and calling. As usual, Heidi was soon surrounded by the goats, who also seemed happy to be back on the Alp.'
6	B	Refer to lines 30-31: 'Heidi immediately recognized Clara's handwriting…'
7	D	Refer to the context of Heidi's reading of the letter. The only two other characters present are Heidi's grandfather and Peter.
8	D	Refer to line 38: 'If you only knew how [the doctor] enjoyed being with you last fall!' 'Fall' and 'autumn' are synonyms.
9	E	Reader's logical inference required. The doctor is visiting Clara every day so it is clear she is not well, and Clara says in her letter: '[the doctor] said that it was so quiet in the pure, delicious air, away from towns and streets, that everybody has to get well there...' (lines 40-41) Therefore, the best option is E: to improve her health.
10	D	Reader's personal judgement required. Clara finishes her letter 'Good-bye, dear Heidi, with much love from grandmama, I am your true friend, Clara' (lines 52-53), and the passage says 'When Peter heard this, he swung his rod to right and left. Furiously driving the goats before him, he bounded down the hill' (lines 54-55). The most likely option is that he is jealous.
11	B	Reader's logical inference. Refer to lines 65-66: 'Give me your hand, for I want to be sure that you are still here.'
12	A	Reader's personal judgement. Refer to line 68: 'The grandmother had hardly slept all night for thinking of Clara's coming.'
13	C	Knowledge of vocabulary required. 'Decided' means having made up one's mind, which is a synonym for 'resolved'. Therefore, the best option is C: decided.
14	D	Knowledge of vocabulary required. Firmament means the sky or heavens. Therefore, the best option is D: heavens.
15	C	Reader's logical inference required. Look at the passage as a whole to make a decision. The narrative is from Heidi's perspective, so this is a good indication that she is the main character.

Test 4 - King Solomon's Mines, pages 25-32

Question	Answer	Explanation
1	B	Refer to line 1: 'Let the reader picture…'
2	C	Refer to lines 4-5: '…[the reader] will get some idea of the size of the enormous cave in which we found ourselves…'
3	A	Reader's personal judgement required. Refer to lines 8-9 'It is impossible for me to convey any idea of the overpowering beauty and grandeur of these pillars…' and lines 17-19 'it would be an interesting calculation to discover how long, at that rate of dripping, it would take to form a pillar' Here the narrator refers to aspects of the cave that he is interested in and curious about, and which also fill him with awe.
4	B	Knowledge of vocabulary required. 'Lofty' means elevated or of imposing height. Therefore, the best option is B: soaring.
5	E	Refer to lines 21-22: 'Cut on one of these pillars we discovered the crude likeness of a mummy, by the head of which sat what appeared to be the figure of an Egyptian god…'
6	A	Reader's logical inference required. Refer to line 29: '…a rate of growth of a foot to a thousand years, or an inch and a fraction to a century.' Multiply 'an inch and a fraction' by three to give just over three inches.
7	D	Refer to lines 31-34: '…the stalagmites took strange forms… one huge mass….was in the shape of a pulpit… Others resembled strange beasts…'
8	B	Knowledge of vocabulary required. 'Irrespective of' means not taking something into account, which is the same as 'regardless of'. Therefore, the best option is B: regardless of.
9	E	Reader's personal judgement required. The narrator describes Gagool as 'our uncanny guide' (line 51), which suggests that she is strange and mysterious, and Gagool asked a question in lines 55-56 'evidently with a view to making [the narrator] feel uncomfortable', which suggests malice.
10	C	Knowledge of vocabulary required. 'Concerned' means troubled or anxious, which is the opposite of 'indifferent'. Therefore, the best option is C: concerned.
11	B	Refer to lines 46-47: '…I was anxious to discover by what system the light was admitted into the cave…'
12	D	Refer to lines 52-54: '…we found another doorway, not arched as the first was, but square at the top, like the doorways of Egyptian temples.'
13	D	Refer to lines 60-61: '"This is getting rather ghastly," said Sir Henry… "Come on, Quatermain… We mustn't keep the old lady waiting!" and he politely made way for me to lead…'
14	C	Reader's logical inference required. The word 'seniores' sounds like 'senior', which means older, and the word 'priores' sounds like 'priority', which has to do with being allowed to go first. Therefore, the most likely translation is 'elders (seniores) first (priores)' (line 61).
15	D	Reader's personal judgement required. Refer to the passage as a whole to form an opinion. The most likely option is D: an adventure story, because the characters are involved in an exhibition/discovery.

Test 5 - Pollyanna, pages 33-40

Question	Answer	Explanation
1	C	Reader's personal judgement required. Refer to lines 1-3: 'The room contained a small bed, neatly made, two straight-backed chairs, a washstand, a bureau – without any mirror – and a small table. There were no drapery curtains at the dormer windows, no pictures on the wall.' This suggests Miss Polly is thrifty. The word 'thrifty' here means using money and resources carefully.
2	A	Reader's logical inference required. Pollyanna's hair is described as 'light' in line 14.
3	E	Knowledge of vocabulary required. 'Sufficient' means adequate, which is the same as 'enough'. Therefore, the best option is E: enough.
4	B	Knowledge of grammar required. An adverb is a word that describes an adjective or a verb. The word in the given phrase that does this is 'crisply', which here describes how something was 'said'.
5	B	Reader's personal judgement required. After Nancy does this, she says '"Light hair, red-checked gingham dress, and straw hat'—all she knows, indeed! Well, I'd be ashamed ter own it up, that I would, I would—and her my onliest niece what was a-comin' from 'way across the continent!' (lines 22-24) This indicates that she is annoyed with Miss Polly because she does not know any personal details about her own niece, so the best option is B.
6	D	Reader's logical inference required. To be someone's 'right-hand man' means to be their 'chief assistant', so the implication of this phrase is that Old Tom is Miss Polly's chief assistant, and Timothy is also an important assistant to Miss Polly.
7	A	Reader's personal judgement required. Timothy responds to Nancy's comment by saying 'Well, if she ain't, nobody knows what'll become of the rest of us… Imagine Miss Polly and a NOISY kid!' (lines 38-39), which suggests Pollyanna needs to be quiet to fit in well in Miss Polly's household.
8	E	Knowledge of vocabulary required. 'Sauntered' means moved in a slow, relaxed manner, which is the opposite of 'rushed'. Therefore, the best option is E: rushed.
9	E	Knowledge of grammar required. An exclamation is a remark expressing surprise or a strong emotion, which fits the role of 'Gorry' in line 39: '"Imagine Miss Polly and a NOISY kid! Gorry! there goes the whistle!"'
10	A	Refer to lines 44-45: 'Beneath the straw hat, an eager, freckled little face turned right and left, plainly searching for some one.'
11	C	Reader's personal judgement required. Pollyanna's continuous flow of cheerful comments from lines 62 to 69 tells us she is enthusiastic and chatty.
12	B	Reader's personal judgement required. The sentence is fondly mocking Pollyanna's incessant chatter, so the best option is B: amusing.
13	C	Knowledge of vocabulary required. 'Ensconced' means established in a comfortable place, which is the same as 'settled'. Therefore, the best option is C: settled.
14	D	Reader's logical inference. Refer to lines 75-77: '…the little girl had kept up an uninterrupted stream of comments and questions, until the somewhat dazed Nancy found herself quite out of breath trying to keep up with her.'
15	A	Reader's logical inference required. The fact that the main character of the story is a child suggests that the passage is from a children's fiction book.

Test 6 - The Woman in White, pages 41-48

Question	Answer	Explanation
1	C	Reader's logical inference required. Refer to lines 1-2: 'The heat had been painfully oppressive all day, and it was now a close and sultry night.' From the description of the heat, we can infer that it is summer.
2	D	Refer to lines 3-5: 'My mother and sister had spoken so many last words, and had begged me to wait another five minutes so many times, that it was nearly midnight when the servant locked the garden-gate behind me.'
3	D	Reader's personal judgement required. The heat is described as 'painfully oppressive' (line 1), which means 'stifling', and we know the sky is clear, and not sunny, because the 'moon was full and broad in the dark blue starless sky…' (line 6)
4	B	Refer to lines 11-12: '…in my present restless frame of mind and body…'
5	E	Knowledge of vocabulary required. 'Heavenly' means wonderful or very pleasing, which is the same as 'divine'. Therefore, the best option is E: heavenly
6	E	Refer to lines 19-21: 'So long as I was proceeding through this first and prettiest part of my night walk my mind remained passively open to the impressions produced by the view; and I thought but little on any subject…'
7	C	Refer to lines 27-30: '…I had become completely absorbed in my own fanciful visions…of the two ladies whose practice in the art of water-colour painting I was so soon to superintend.'
8	E	Refer to line 31: 'I had now arrived at that particular point of my walk where four roads met…'
9	D	Refer to line 46: The woman in white asks the narrator where the road to London is (line 46), which indicates that she is trying to find her way.
10	C	Refer to lines 57-58: 'Her figure was slight, and rather above the average height…'
11	A	Reader's personal judgement required. Given that it is as if she had 'dropped from heaven' (line 40), the best description is A: she is mysterious and possibly magical.
12	E	Refer to line 65: The woman asks the narrator if he heard her before she repeats her question (line 65).
13	B	Knowledge of grammar required. 'Fretfulness' is the state of feeling distressed, so it is an abstract noun, which is a noun denoting a quality or state rather than a physical thing.
14	B	Refer to lines 76-77: 'I only wondered at your appearance in the road, because it seemed to me to be empty the instant before I saw you.'
15	D	Reader's personal judgement required. Given the mysterious appearance of the woman in the middle of the road and the confusion of the narrator, it is mostly likely that the passage belongs to a mystery story.

Test 7 - The Secret Garden, pages 49-56

Question	Answer	Explanation
1	E	Refer to line 1: 'The sun shone down for nearly a week on the secret garden.'
2	C	Refer to lines 1-4: 'The Secret Garden was what Mary called it when she was thinking of it. She liked the name, and she liked still more the feeling that when its beautiful old walls shut her in no one knew where she was.'
3	D	Refer to lines 8-10: '…every day which passed at Misselthwaite. She was beginning to like to be out of doors; she no longer hated the wind…'
4	C	Refer to line 10-11: '[Mary] could run faster, and longer, and she could skip up to a hundred.'
5	B	Knowledge of literary techniques required. Personification is attributing human characteristics to non-human things. We see this in the description, '…they barely peeped above the earth' (line 23).
6	D	'Mary' and 'person' are nouns. 'Was' is a verb. 'An' is a determiner. 'Odd', 'determined' and 'little' are adjectives. Therefore, four word classes are used in this sentence.
7	A	Reader's logical inference required. Refer to lines 20-25: '[Mary] found many more of the sprouting pale green points than she had ever hoped to find… There were so many that she remembered what Martha had said about…bulbs spreading and making new ones.'
8	B	Reader's personal judgement required. Refer to lines 32-36: '…she was afraid that he would pick up his tools and go away if he saw her coming, so she always walked toward him as silently as possible. But, in fact, he did not object to her as strongly as he had at first. Perhaps he was secretly rather flattered by her evident desire for his elderly company. Then, also, she was more civil than she had been.' This suggests that they have recently grown closer.
9	A	Reader's logical inference required. Ben clearly works in the garden and is referred to as 'pick[ing] up his tools' (line 32) and as 'rest[ing] one hobnailed boot on the top of his spade' (lines 47-48), which suggests he is a gardener.
10	E	Refer to lines 39-41: 'Tha'rt like th' robin… I never knows when I shall see thee or which side tha'll come from.'
11	A	Reader's personal judgement required. Refer to lines 60-61: '…he flirted his wings and tail and tilted his head and hopped about with all sorts of lively graces.' This suggests that he is plucky because he is venturing near Ben and cheeky because he is hopping about.
12	B	Refer to lines 65-67: 'I know what tha's up to. Tha's courtin' some bold young madam somewhere, tellin' thy lies to her about bein' th' finest cock robin on Missel Moor an' ready to fight all th' rest of 'em.'
13	D	Refer to lines 70-71: 'He flew on to the nearest currant bush and tilted his head and sang a little song right at him.'
14	E	Reader's logical inference required. Refer to lines 77-78: 'He stood still as if he were afraid to breathe…' This suggests he is feeling awe.
15	D	Ben is referred to as a 'Yorkshire man' (line 38), and the way in which his speech is written is suggestive of a Yorkshire accent.

Test 8 - Tarzan and the Apes, pages 57-64

Question	Answer	Explanation
1	C	Refer to lines 2-4: '[Tarzan} saw that at one point the forest touched the village, and to this spot he made his way, lured by a fever of curiosity to behold animals of his own kind, and to learn more of their ways and view the strange lairs in which they lived.'
2	A	Reader's logical inference required. Refer to lines 1-5 to help make a decision as the meaning of the word 'brutes'. Tarzan is referred to as living among 'the brutes of the jungle' (line 5). He is also 'lured by a fever of curiosity to behold animals of his own kind' (line 3) for the first time, who are living in a village in thatched huts and are clearly human. Therefore, the only logical option, especially in view of the title of the story, is that the brutes are animals.
3	E	Knowledge of vocabulary required. The word 'erroneous' means 'incorrect'. Therefore, the best option is E: correct.
4	E	Refer to lines 12-23: 'Few were [Tarzan's] primitive pleasures, but the greatest of these was to hunt and kill…'
5	D	Reader's logical inference required. Refer to lines 16-18: '[Tarzan's] strange life had left him neither morose nor bloodthirsty… that he killed with a joyous laugh upon his handsome lips betokened no innate cruelty…' Tarzan is described as handsome and as enjoying the athletic activity of hunting, without excess enjoyment of cruelty.
6	C	Refer to line 18: 'Tarzan] killed for food most often…'
7	A	Reader's logical inference required. The passage states 'Kulonga had taught him great respect for the little sharp splinters of wood' (line 25-26) and that Tarzan 'knew nothing of the brotherhood of man. All things outside his own tribe were his deadly enemies…'(lines 9-10). It can be inferred that Kulonga must belong to Tarzan's tribe, as he teaches Tarzan. As Tarzan's name is 'Tarzan of the Apes', Kulonga must be an ape.
8	A	Reader's logical inference required. Refer to lines 49-59 to help make a decision as to what 'sharp splinters of wood' (lines 25-26) refers to. The weapons are referred to as 'tiny missiles' (line 50), as a 'little arrow' (line 55) and as 'death-dealing slivers' (line 57). From these descriptions it can be inferred that these weapons are very small projectiles. Therefore, the most appropriate option would be A: darts.
9	E	Reader's logical inference required. Refer to lines 27-28 'At length [Tarzan] came to a great tree, heavy laden with thick foliage and loaded with pendant loops of giant creepers' to help make a decision as to the meaning of the phrase 'impenetrable bower' (line 28). It can be inferred that Tarzan is covered by the heavy foliage of the tree and so is concealed from view from those beneath him.
10	E	Refer to lines 31-34: 'There were women grinding dried plantain in crude stone mortars, while others were fashioning cakes from the powdered flour. Out in the fields he could see still other women hoeing, weeding, or gathering.'
11	B	Refer to lines 35-37: 'many were loaded with brass and copper anklets, armlets and bracelets. Around many a dusky neck hung curiously coiled strands of wire, while several were further ornamented by huge nose rings.'
12	A	Reader's personal judgement required. Refer to lines 49-59 to help form an opinion of how Tarzan is feeling. The passage states that 'Tarzan was fascinated. Here was the secret of the terrible destructiveness of The Archer's tiny missiles' (lines 49-50) and that 'he should like to have more of those little death-dealing slivers' (lines 56-57). It can be inferred, therefore, that Tarzan is excited about the prospect of the poison weapons.
13	E	Refer to line 68: 'Tarzan knew they had found the body of his victim…'
14	A	Knowledge of vocabulary required. The word 'motionless' means 'immobile', which both refer to not moving.
15	C	Reader's logical inference required. Refer to the passage as a whole to make a decision. Tarzan is especially unique because he lives in a tribe of apes.

Test 9 - The Happy Prince, pages 65-70

Question	Answer	Explanation
1	B	Knowledge of vocabulary required. Sapphires are precious stones, usually of a bright blue colour. Therefore, the best option is B: jewels.
2	A	Reader's personal judgement required. Refer to lines 4-6: '"He is as beautiful as a weathercock," remarked one of the Town Councillors who wished to gain a reputation for having artistic tastes.'
3	E	Knowledge of vocabulary required. A weathercock is a revolving metal pointer indicating the direction of the wind.
4	A	Reader's logical inference required. Refer to lines 8-10 to help make a decision as to why the mother wants her son to be more like the Happy Prince specifically. She says: '"Why can't you be like the Happy Prince?" ... "The Happy Prince never dreams of crying for anything."' It can inferred that she wishes her child to be happier, like the statue.
5	D	Refer to line 14: '…in their bright scarlet cloaks…'
6	C	Refer to lines 19-20: 'he had stayed behind, for he was in love with the most beautiful Reed.' A reed is a plant which grows in or nearby water.
7	D	Refer to lines 27-28: '"It is a ridiculous attachment," twittered the other Swallows; "she has no money, and far too many relations."'
8	A	Knowledge of vocabulary required. 'Landed' means to come down from the air and rest on a surface, and 'alighted' means to descend from the air and land. Therefore, the best option is A: landed.
9	B	Knowledge of vocabulary required. 'Curious' in the context of the passage means strange, unusual or odd, rather than inquisitive or nosey. Therefore, the best option is B: strange.
10	E	Reader's logical inference required. Refer to lines 46-47 'The climate in the north of Europe…' to help make a decision as to where this story is most likely set. The only country in the list of answer option which is in the north of Europe is Germany.
11	E	Reader's personal judgement required. Refer to lines 62-65: '"Round the garden ran a very lofty wall, but I never cared to ask what lay beyond it, everything about me was so beautiful. My courtiers called me the Happy Prince, and happy indeed I was, if pleasure be happiness."'
12	B	Refer to line 69: '…a low musical voice…'
13	C	Refer to line 72: '…she is a seamstress.'
14	E	Reader's personal judgement required. Refer to lines 56-58: '"So I lived, and so I died. And now that I am dead they have set me up here so high that I can see all the ugliness and all the misery of my city, and though my heart is made of lead yet I cannot choose but weep."' The implication is that the Prince feels guilty about being unaware of other people's suffering before and now wants to make up for this indifference.
15	C	Refer to line 77: 'My feet are fastened to this pedestal and I cannot move.'

Test 10 - The Prisoner of Zenda, pages 71-78

Question	Answer	Explanation
1	B	Reader's logical inference required. Refer to line 1 to make a decision as to the time of day: 'I took an early luncheon…' If the narrator's lunchtime is considered 'early' it can be inferred that he is eating before the afternoon.
2	C	Refer to lines 3-4: 'Half an hour's leisurely walking brought me to the Castle.'
3	A	Refer to lines 8-9: 'The old and the new portions were connected by a drawbridge…'
4	A	Refer to line 7: '…a handsome modern chateau, erected by the last king…'
5	B	Knowledge of vocabulary required. 'Sombre' means dark, dull or serious. The word 'bright' means light or vivid. Therefore, this is the word with the most opposite meaning.
6	E	Reader's personal judgement required. Refer to lines 18-19 to form an opinion as to why the narrator compares the sunlight to diamonds specifically. He notes that 'the sunshine stole through in patches as bright as diamonds, and hardly bigger.' He refers to the brightness of the two things that he is comparing, so E is the best option.
7	B	Refer to lines 26-27: '…I fell to dreaming that I was married to the Princess Flavia and dwelt in the Castle of Zenda…'
8	A	Knowledge of vocabulary required. 'Fanciful' means unrealistic and imaginative, and 'whimsical' means unrealistic in an amusing way. Therefore, the best option is A: fanciful.
9	E	Reader's logical inference required. Refer to lines 40-42 to make a decision as to what the two men have in common. The narrator notes that he 'set the one down as an old soldier: the other for a gentleman accustomed to move in good society, but not unused to military life either. It turned out afterwards that [his] guess was a good one.' The narrator is right in his assumption that two are both in the army.
10	B	Reader's logical inference required. Refer to line 53: 'I bowed and, baring my head, answered…' As the narrator is bowing to his new acquaintances at the same time as baring his head, the most logical option is that he is taking his hat off in greeting.
11	D	Reader's logical inference required. Refer to lines 51-52 to make a decision as to where this passage is set. The two men in the forest described themselves as being 'in the service of the King of Ruritania' and as this king appears later in the passage it can be inferred that this is where the story is set.
12	D	Reader's logical inference required. Refer to the passage as a whole to help make a decision as to which answer option does not describe the narrator. The narrator describes himself as being 'six feet two inches' (lines 45-46) Therefore, the only option which is false is D: that he is short.
13	C	Reader's logical inference required. Refer to lines 79-82: 'Saving the hair on my face and a manner of conscious dignity which his position gave him…the King of Ruritania might have been Rudolf Rassendyll, and I, Rudolf, the King.' This description implies that the two men are similar in appearance.
14	A	Reader's logical inference required. Look at the passage as a whole to make a decision. The passage is written from the point of view of Rudolf Rassendyll, so it can be assumed that he is the main character.
15	E	Reader's personal judgement required. The passage is most likely from a fictitious novel, as it talks of fictitious countries, and there is no indication that it is funny or of anything fantastical, which only leaves option E: adventure.

Other Titles in the First Past The Post® Series

English: Comprehensions

All books in this series contain 10 tests, each comprising a long passage with 15 accompanying questions. These tests are designed to be representative of the standard comprehension section of contemporary multi-discipline 11 plus and Common Entrance exams. Questions test the student's ability to extract factual information or draw inferences from the text, and some test the student's knowledge of vocabulary, grammar or literary techniques. All questions are multiple-choice, and full answers and explanations are included. Each book allows access to our Peer-Compare™ Online system, which assesses the candidate's performance anonymously on a question-by-question basis.

Classic Literature

All 10 passages in these books are taken from classic fiction books, such as those by Charles Dickens and Louisa May Alcott. These passages contain more challenging vocabulary than modern literature.

Contemporary Literature

All 10 passages in these books are written in the style of modern fiction books, using contemporary vocabulary.

Non-Fiction

All 10 passages in these books are modern non-fiction pieces, such as opinion pieces, reviews and journal articles.

Other Titles in the First Past The Post® Series

English: Mini-Comprehensions

All books in this series contain 50 exercises, each of which comprises a short passage with six accompanying questions. The aim of these books is to focus on specific question types typically found in the standard comprehension section of contemporary multi-discipline 11 plus and Common Entrance exams: inference questions and fact-finding questions. Each book contains 35 fiction passages and 15 non-fiction passages, and all questions are in standard format. Full answers and explanations are included.

Inference

Inference questions are those which require the candidate to read more deeply into the text to infer the answers from the details given. Answers to these questions are not explicitly stated in the passage. For example, a candidate may be asked how a character is feeling or why a character made a certain action.

Fact-Finding

Answers to fact-finding questions are always explicitly stated in the text, so candidates should be able to answer these questions without any inference or judgement. For example, a candidate might be asked what colour an object is or how old a character is.

Other Titles in the First Past The Post® Series

English: Spelling, Punctuation & Grammar

These books provide focused practice for spelling, punctuation & grammar. These question styles are tailored towards the last section of the Granada Learning (GL) English assessment, and are designed to test knowledge of the English language. Each book contains 15 spelling exercises, 15 punctuation exercises, 15 grammar exercises and three mixed tests. Each mixed test contains all question types and is designed to provide timed practice. Full answers and explanations are included.

Each exercise comprises a short passage or series of sentences, including a range of classic fiction, contemporary fiction and non-fiction pieces. Candidates must find the spelling or punctuation error on each line, or select the correct word from the options provided so that the sentence makes grammatical sense.

Other Titles in the First Past The Post® Series

English: Practice Papers (GL)

These books provide real exam practice via four timed tests. These are tailored towards the Granada Learning (GL) English assessments but provide invaluable practice for all exam boards. Each test comprises a comprehension section and a spelling, punctuation and grammar section, reflecting the likely make-up of the real exam. Full answers and explanations are included.

Each test can be marked and evaluated via our Peer-Compare™ Online system, which assesses the candidate's performance anonymously on a question-by-question basis. This helps identify areas for improvement and benchmarks the candidate's score against that of others who have taken the same tests.

Other Titles in the First Past The Post® Series

Creative Writing: Examples

These books provide examples of peer-written passages, each accompanied by an activity which helps deepen the candidate's understanding of the requirements of the exam. The pages are brightly coloured, with fun pictures and child-friendly workspaces. This series is indispensable for improving creative writing skills, with hints on how to create a good structure, how to plan and how to use great descriptive language.

This workbook contains 33 peer-written pieces, each accompanied by activities, checklists and teacher's comments. Examples of typical exam questions are also included, designed to help candidates create a story in no more than 30 minutes, including five minutes to plan.